WRITING
NON-FICTION
BOOKS

The Essential Guide

D1493083

Need
— 2 —
Know

First published by Macmillan Publishers Ltd/Papermac in 1981
(with a minimally revised edition in 1989)
as *The Successful Author's Handbook*

Completely revised and rewritten – but following the same sequence and principles
– and published by Allison & Busby Ltd in 1996 as *How to Write Non-fiction Books*

Completely revised, updated – and condensed – edition published
in Great Britain in 1999 by Writers' Bookshop.
Writers' Bookshop is an imprint of Forward Press Ltd.

This new revised edition is published in Great Britain in 2010 by
Need2Know
Remus House
Coltsfoot Drive
Peterborough
PE2 9JX
Telephone 01733 898103
Fax 01733 313524
www.need2knowbooks.co.uk

Need2Know is an imprint of Forward Press Ltd.
www.forwardpress.co.uk

Contents

Introduction

Many long to write a book. They dream of having a book on their shelves with their name on the cover.

Too many dream of that book being a novel. The competition for publication of a first novel is fierce, and it's not as easy as it looks to tell a good and commercially viable story. Few earn the vast sums reportedly paid to the big names in popular fiction.

But there are also non-fiction books.

Tens of thousands of new books are published each year in Britain alone and the proportion of non-fiction to fiction is at least six to one. There are more opportunities for non-fiction books than there are for novels and the competition is less; there are more aspiring novelists than non-fiction writers.

Writing a non-fiction book is every bit as worthy an occupation as writing a novel and is more likely to achieve success. Many people think vaguely about writing a book on their particular interest; few actually get down to working on it; fewer still complete the task. It entails a lot of hard work. And there is a right way and a wrong way to go about it.

This book will tell you how to do it the right way.

'The first thing to learn is that you will almost certainly have to write your book the way a publisher wants it.'

The professional approach

The first thing to learn is that you will almost certainly have to write your book the way a publisher wants it, which may not be the way you first think of it.

It is often advantageous for a non-fiction book to fit into a publisher's existing series. It may need to be written to a specific length or directed at a slightly different readership than you propose. It is therefore important not to start writing your book too soon.

That's so important, it's worth repeating and emphasising:

Don't start writing your book yet!

A non-fiction book has to be carefully planned; its content needs to be organised; you may even need to think about the eventual layout of the book pages. In all these matters, it is best to sound out the views and requirements of the eventual publisher before doing too much writing. It is wisest to adopt a professional approach.

The professional approach to non-fiction book writing can be thought of as 10 steps (see opposite).

The non-fiction author should get a publisher's firm commitment to the proposed book before much of it is written. It is customary for a publisher to sign an agreement with a non-fiction author – even a first-time author – on the basis of a synopsis and sample chapters. Many agreements provide for a partial advance against royalties. In other words, the non-fiction author gets some money 'up front'.

Write to sell

Now, motivation. Why do you want to write this book? Money? You would probably do better cleaning windows or stacking supermarket shelves. Status, kudos, recognition? These factors can certainly be an important part of your reason for writing, just as money too can be a part. But neither money nor kudos should be the main reason for writing your book. On their own they are likely to lead to unenthusiastic 'hack' writing.

If you are going to write a book, you must believe that there is a need for it; that you can produce something that others will find useful, interesting and of value. You must enjoy the writing too, the organising, the careful stringing together of the words. In other words, you can't not write your book.

Your conviction that there is a need for your book, and your personal need to write it, will be accompanied by the supporting prospect of money and kudos. Altogether, they amount to a believable reason for writing it. (Beware though of a conceited or over-inflated view of your own ability.)

Yet all these reasons for writing must be subjugated to the requirements of the marketplace. You must write what the customer wants. All the time you are writing your non-fiction book you must think of the needs of the reader, which means that first you have to identify your reader.

1. Define the subject of your book. Bear in mind your own knowledge and experience, your ability to cover the whole subject (or redefine it so that you can) and your ability to gain access to the material you will need.

2. Assess the market for the book. Think about the readership you hope to address and the competition. Identify a gap in the market; some way in which you can write your book so that it will differ from and be better than its competitors. Identify the publishers most likely to be interested in your book.

3. Think about further subject research. Almost certainly you will need to undertake more research.

4. Prepare a sales package (my term for the material with which you will seek to interest a publisher). This will consist of a detailed synopsis and a statement of the book's purpose, its potential market, how it will differ from its competitors and why you are the ideal author.

5. Interest a publisher in your proposal with your sales package. Be prepared to discuss and adjust the synopsis (and possibly the target readership) to an interested publisher's requirements. Be flexible.

6. Write one or two sample chapters. Ideally have them almost ready before discussions with the publisher. They should not exceed about 20% of the total book.

7. Negotiate and sign an agreement with the publisher before you write any more of the book.

Your book is sold. All you have to do now is…

8. Write the book. Work to the agreed synopsis and, ideally, to a word budget and timetable.

9. Deliver the completed book manuscript.

10. Help the publisher to sell the book.

The world of publishing

First-time writers of non-fiction sometimes find it irksome to adjust what they want to write to fit the needs of the reader as represented by the publisher. But unless there are readers, you won't be communicating.

The plus side of the coin is that if there is a need (and room) for your book in the market and if it's any good, you will find someone to publish it for you. There are hundreds of publishers in Britain alone; without new books to publish they will go out of business. Publishers need new books to produce those tens of thousands of new titles each year. But they're in business and must make a profit to survive; they will only take on commercially viable propositions.

Major publishers need books that will sell nationally and, even better, internationally. There are also many smaller publishers who will consider books of local or specialist interest.

To repeat, if there is a market for your book, and if it's any good, someone will publish it for you.

'If you are going to write a book, you must believe that there is a need for it.'

Let me clarify. The phrase 'will publish it for you' means the author supplies the text (and illustrations as appropriate) and the publisher converts the pages of typescript into printed books and markets them entirely at his own expense. The publisher pays the author, usually a percentage of the sales figures or sometimes a lump sum payment. Authors do not pay publishers. If a publisher asks you to pay, back off fast.

Very occasionally, a reputable publisher will seek to negotiate sponsorship (or subsidy) for a book. The book could, for example, be the history of a large organisation that might agree to pay part of the cost of publication in order to hold down the sale price. However, such subsidies almost always come after – and do not influence – the 'literary' acceptability of the book.

It is necessary to explain the normal world of publishing in order to comment on the alternatives: self-publishing and so-called 'vanity publishing'.

Self-publishing

Self-publishing is sometimes a practical alternative to conventional publishing. It is often the only course of action for authors of books of extremely narrow specialism or local interest. It may be the right thing for a village history or a 'how to' book about a small-interest hobby or craft. (It is often the only way for a poet to achieve publication.)

However, self-publishing should never be the automatic recourse of an author seeking to avoid the editorial changes asked for by a commercially minded conventional publisher. Changes for commercial reasons are usually worth making.

But let me define self-publishing. The self-publishing author:

- Writes a book.
- Decides that it warrants publication.
- Finances the entire publication of the book.
- Edits it (or pays a professional editor to edit it).
- Designs and typesets the pages (or pays someone else to do it).
- Negotiates with a printer for the book production.
- Arranges for the marketing of the book (publicity, selling to bookshops, etc).

'If there is a market for your book, and if it's any good, someone will publish it for you.'

All of the above is possible and, where the author knows the book's potential market well (the villagers and the local bookshops, or relevant specialist magazines and organisations), practical too. But it entails the investment of much of the author's time and money.

The help list at the back of this book includes details of ProPrint, a publisher who handles self-publishing for authors.

Without doubt, self-publishing is a viable proposition for any author of a narrow-interest, ultra-specialist, non-fiction book. But don't go into it without your eyes wide open: it's a lot of non-writing work and can eat up capital. Try to find a 'proper' publisher first, before going down the self-publishing road.

Vanity publishing

Vanity publishing is different and is to be avoided at all costs. It gets its name from the way in which virtually every manuscript offered to the 'publisher' is deemed worthy of acceptance and publication.

Vanity publishers are not hard to identify. They advertise for writers with a book 'that merits publication' or suchlike. They sometimes tell you, in their advertisements, that they are 'shared-cost' or 'joint-venture' publishers. Whatever they may tell you, your 'share' of the usually excessive costs will be far from equal and certainly not fair. Vanity publishers' profits come entirely from your 'contribution'.

No reputable publisher needs to advertise for books; they are usually swamped with unsolicited manuscripts – mostly unsuitable. A real publisher stakes his money and his professional reputation on each book that he publishes under his imprint. Vanity publishers are singularly unselective in what they accept for publication. They'll praise and publish anything – because you're paying.

Vanity publishers seldom produce more than a few bound copies of their books. They may print more sheet-copies, but these are seldom bound. These 'publishers' are often little more than jobbing printers, and print run-ons are not costly.

If a publisher advertises for authors and then seeks a financial contribution towards the cost of publication as a condition of acceptance, run for cover. This is shark-infested territory.

The variety of non-fiction books

There are many varieties of non-fiction book. It is convenient to classify them under two broad headings: those that are basically 'technical' and those that are basically 'story-line'. There are, as we shall explain later, differences in the way these two non-fiction categories should be handled. Let me explain and define the two general categories.

I classify as technical non-fiction books:

- All textbooks, irrespective of subject, from the 'purest' art to the 'purest' science via technology of all kinds, and irrespective of target readership level, from preschool toddler to postgraduate professor.

- All 'how to' books. Again, being textbooks in all but name, irrespective of subject (craft, hobby, sport, pastime, work-skill, etc) and target readership.

- All 'collecting' books for all levels of readership, about all types of collectibles; from birds' eggs and porcelain figurines, to pop records and garden gnomes and even collected information – reference books.

Under the broad heading of story-line non-fiction books, I would include:

- Biographies and autobiographies of all types and readership levels, from the brief, personal-experience account of an 'ordinary person's' unusual or amusing week/month/year, to the heavyweight biography of a major historical or political character.

- All histories, for example of a five-day war, of the struggle for control of a commercial company, of a sports club or organisation, of a sporting competition or even the story of the universe from start to present-day – again, at all readership levels.

- Books about social policies such as the thoughts of a leading politician.

- Books about travellers' experiences, as opposed to guidebooks, which I would classify as technical.

And I think, purely because they would probably be treated in a similar fashion, I would also include here the odd one out:

- Books of humour.

My non-fiction categorisation is a broad, subjective approach. You may wonder where a particular book of yours fits into this scheme of things. Don't worry. There are differences in the way you move your book forward, but these differences are mainly in the way you approach the publishers. No publisher is going to reject a book because your approach is slightly unusual. If the idea is good, the publisher will ask for anything he thinks is missing.

For the avoidance of doubt and confusion throughout the rest of this book, I shall refer to publishers as male and editors as female. The terms and comments are equally appropriate to female publishers and male editors. I'm not sexist, just a lazy writer.

Chapter One

The Basic Idea

So, you have decided to write a non-fiction book. Let's think a little more about the types of non-fiction book.

Many aspiring authors immediately think of writing about themselves. They think, wrongly, that this will be an easy book to write. They think that people will be interested in the story of their eventful lives. Wrong again.

Are you already famous or are your experiences sufficiently unusual, newsworthy or funny to generate the necessary '15 minutes' of fame? Unless you tick these boxes, or are writing solely for your own family's consumption, don't write your memoirs.

The only other justification for writing about yourself is when you believe – and can persuade a publisher – that others can learn from your experiences. (Excellent examples of such light autobiographies are the testimonies published by the religious presses. They encourage others down a similar path.)

Biographies of well-known personalities are certainly a possibility. The 'ordinary' writer, though, should usually avoid the 'heavyweight' historical biography; academic writers will jealously guard their inside track on such books. There is some scope for established writers to 'ghost' the autobiographies of others, but this is no job for anyone without a track record. Similarly, to write an entertainment world biography it's almost essential to have inside contacts.

Generally, there are more opportunities for a non-fiction book in the broadly defined technical area. Whether technical or story-line though, you must define the subject.

'There are more opportunities for a non-fiction book in the broadly defined technical area.'

A book about what?

Some know a lot about their job or hobby; some are enthusiastic about a sport or game; some are interested in the arts or have healthcare experience; some collect artefacts, others information. Many people have some knowledge or experience that can be shared with others. Identify your own subject.

Write down as concisely as possible the subject you propose to write about. Now think more about this subject. If you are to write a book about something, you must know the subject well.

Break the subject down into sub-topics. These can be periods in a person's life, stages in a process, aspects of a game (e.g. training, rules, tactics, etc), alternative ways of achieving an end, and so on. Do you know enough about each of these sub-topics to write about them in depth? Have you just divided the subject into those aspects of which you are well aware, or is it really a comprehensive coverage of the subject? Are you thinking about the whole subject or just the part that interests you?

It is not necessarily wrong to restrict a subject to those parts that interest you. But you must be sure that the restricted subject can stand alone, logically, and in its own right.

A general-interest gardening book could reasonably gloss over the science of soil chemistry. The ordinary gardener doesn't need to know. However, it could not exclude advice on planting timetables or fertiliser requirements. But the whole subject of practical gardening could be narrowed down. There could be books on the small city garden, gardening for those with little time (*The Hour-a-Week Gardener* sounds good to me) or growing delphiniums. Such refining of a subject is perfectly acceptable. Indeed, it is often the best way of finding a suitable book subject.

Don't narrow your subject down too far, though. It must be sufficient to warrant a book about it.

Demand and scope

It is not enough, though, merely to consider whether a subject is big enough to write about. Is the subject one that people will want to buy a book about? How many people? You may be the world's leading expert on double-ended oojimaflips and have much to write about them – but is anyone else in the world interested in them?

Even the most specialist of publishers will hope to sell a couple of thousand copies of any book published, and many of these sales could be to libraries, which implies multiple readership. You need to think of a subject that will appeal to at least several thousand people. The broader the scope of the book, the larger the potential readership.

If your basic idea is too small or too specialist to warrant a book in its own right or attract sufficient readership, broaden its scope.

Maybe you should consider collaboration with another writer. It is sometimes possible to write a book with another specialist, equally as narrow as yourself perhaps, and produce a worthwhile, saleable, joint effort.

If there is only a relatively small – but important – aspect of your chosen subject on which you are not competent to write, you might negotiate with a colleague to write a specific chapter on that aspect for you. (You should reserve the right to edit your colleague's text, subject to a post-edit check, to ensure that it conforms to the style of the rest of the book. It is also best to compensate a one-chapter collaborator with a lump sum payment rather than a share of future royalties.)

Another important factor affecting the demand for the book and influencing the scope and coverage is the educational level at which the book is pitched. The aspiring non-fiction author must consider the needs of the reader at all times. The coverage and treatment will differ widely if the potential reader is a scientist or a school child.

'You need to think of a subject that will appeal to at least several thousand people.'

The competition – other people's books

At this stage in the non-fiction authorship process, while you are still working on the basic idea for your book, you must run a check on the opposition. Unless you are very lucky – or have chosen a too-unusual subject – there will already be several other books on the same subject. You need to investigate as many of them as possible.

If your subject is a specialist one, you may think you know all the competing books; you might be wrong. You must check. If your subject is broad and of general interest, check the competition at the same level as you propose.

Visit your local library. Consult the listings of books on your subject and browse through the relevant sections of the shelves. Glance at all the competing titles and borrow the best. Chat to the librarian, not only about available and competing titles, but also about their relative popularity (check the number of recent date stamps in the front of relevant books too).

Visit your local bookshop and chat to the proprietor – he may know of less directly related titles. Notice which publishers handle your type of book and which, in your view, handle them best (striking covers, good binding, advertising posters, etc) This information will be of use later.

You need to get a feel for the whole of the opposition: the level at which competing books are pitched, the breadth and depth of their coverage, their treatment, and whether, in your view, they are good value for money. If you owned all of the competing books, would you still buy another? Specifically, yours?

If yours is to be a technical type book, you must think about how your book can carve out a new slice of what is a relatively fixed market. Your book will have to sell at the expense of someone else's book. Whose? Why?

If yours is a story-line book, how long ago was its closest competitor published? Is it yet time for the next book?

Your book is obviously going to be better, in some way, than the competition. (If not, why write it?) You must be able to explain why your book is needed – which vacant niche in the wall of information it will fill.

Need2Know

Maybe your book will explain the subject more simply or maybe it will go into more detail about one important aspect of the subject. (Should it perhaps concentrate on that aspect alone?) Maybe new information has become available and, best of all, only to you. Maybe all the existing books seem to be written for American readers and you will be writing for a British readership. Maybe you can identify a group of readers – male, female, teenagers, technicians, etc – not yet, or not adequately, catered for. Or you have found a publisher whose ongoing series lacks a book on the subject you propose. Even if the market is full of children's books on dinosaurs, say, every publisher wants his own book on them. For completeness. (I know: I've written one.)

There always seems to be room for another good book on virtually any subject as long as it is better in some way, or fills a need.

Do not treat lightly or rush this survey of competing books. It is important for two reasons. First, it will give you ideas on how, or how not, to treat the subject in your own book and on the way you will inevitably pick up snippets of new information – it's all useful research (see chapter 2). Secondly, later in the book-writing process, when you have gained the interest of a publisher, he will want to know about the competition and the ways in which your book will be better. He will need to decide how to direct his sales campaign for your book and how to convince those who own the competing books to buy yours too.

You can only answer the publisher's inevitable queries from detailed knowledge. To win, you must know your enemy.

Summing Up

- Unless you are already famous or have done something unusual, don't write about yourself.

- A broad 'how to' book probably stands the best chance of publication – a job, a hobby, a sport, one's health, collecting something – or a textbook. Bear in mind that you can restrict the scope of the book to a portion of the broader subject.

- Give thought to the potential readership. If your subject is of limited appeal, a publisher will be less interested – he needs to sell copies to make his living.

- Check all the other books on the same subject. You will need to explain to the publisher how your book will be better than all the others. If not, why write it?

Chapter Two

Research – Collecting and Organising Material

The most important thing about a non-fiction book is the factual information it conveys. Inaccuracy is a cardinal sin.

The need for research

A non-fiction author has to collect information. The non-fiction author must know all there is to know in their chosen field (subject to the level at which the book is to be written).

This can mean detailed specialised knowledge of a small aspect of a subject, or knowing more than is ordinarily necessary about all aspects of a broad subject.

The non-fiction author must be aware of most, if not all, of the books that have been published in the field. But book learning alone is not enough. The author must be up to date, which means regularly collecting material from magazines and newspapers. The collection of material is an ongoing process.

It is unusual and potentially disastrous to decide on a specialist subject for a non-fiction book and only then, at that stage, to start collecting material.

Select a book subject from 'within reach of' one's existing broad interests. There will always be a need to collect further specific, more detailed material, but this research is best done from a broad foundation of related knowledge. The time-honoured advice 'write about what you know' is certainly well founded. But I would extend it to: 'Know your subject thoroughly before writing about it'.

'Know your subject thoroughly before writing about it.'

The advice about working within existing areas of interest needs elaboration. It is clearly relevant to an idea for a book about 'gold amalgams…' or a mathematics textbook. But what about a book on, say, 'walking in Wales'? You might think that this would entail no more research than to go walking with your eyes open. But to make sense you would need to have some related interests. A keen walker, interested in the breeding habits of the 'lesser spotted chaffinch', the surrounding nature and the background to all those piles of old stones would undoubtedly have a good head start on a couch potato like me. They would know what to look out for.

Don't be frightened by this talk of research. You don't need to reinvent the wheel or rediscover penicillin. Research, to a writer, means the collection and collating of information. It need not entail physical or mental discovery, though of course does not preclude it. A writer does not have to extend the bounds of all human knowledge, merely the knowledge of the reader. The planned level of readership will also influence the amount and depth of the research: a non-fiction book for school children does not entail such detailed research as a graduate text.

Plagiarism and copyright

In the context of their research, some aspiring authors worry about plagiarism and copyright. These matters are important, but they need not be a major constraint.

It was once, flippantly, explained to me that if I consulted just one book before I wrote something, the result probably constituted plagiarism. If I consulted two books, this was legitimate research. This advice may be over-simplistic, but it contains a large measure of common sense.

There can be no copyright of a fact, nor of an idea. Copyright applies to the form in which the fact or idea is expressed. That is, the way in which the words are strung together: direct quotation.

It is not enough to quote the source of a quotation. A credit line does not absolve the 'copying author' of an infringement of copyright. Although any direct quotation is legally an infringement, it is accepted practice that brief quotations may be made for purposes of review or criticism. Brief attributed quotations for purposes other than criticism or review are also often made without the express permission of the copyright owner and, being brief, are usually permitted by default. When in doubt though, a non-fiction author should always seek the permission of the copyright owner for any quotation.

Plagiarism is less easy to define. In academic circles, a technical paper based on the unacknowledged research of another would certainly be plagiarism; if nothing else, the 'author' would be attracting undeserved kudos. In more everyday writing circles, a close and lengthy paraphrase of another's work would be classified as plagiarism. When in doubt, seek permission and generally avoid direct paraphrasing of others' work.

Which brings us back to the flippant introduction to this section: consult a number of research sources, not just one.

Research sources

A non-fiction author cannot survive on book research alone. The non-fiction author must collect both ongoing and specific information for a new book from a variety of sources. These will include:

- Personal observation, experience (own and others') and expertise.
- Original research – questionnaires, interviews and correspondence.
- Odds and ends – ephemera, brochures, radio and TV programmes.
- Material gleaned from journals, magazines, newspapers, etc.
- Books – one's own and those borrowed, e.g. from libraries.

And of course, increasingly important nowadays…

- The Internet – on which there is further information overleaf.

No one source will normally suffice on its own.

Personal observation, experience and expertise are potentially the most valuable research sources available to a non-fiction author. Impossible without involvement, personal experience can lead to committed writing; certainly it ensures detailed knowledge. Experience lets you incorporate personal anecdotes in your writing. This can be extremely valuable.

'Consult a number of research sources, not just one.'

This book is a good example of writing based largely on personal experience. I've been there. I've done it. Often. And survived. (But no t-shirts.)

Over many years of writing non-fiction, I have tried out several different ways of working. Some were good, others less so. I've read many books on non-fiction writing. From them, I've absorbed anything I thought worthwhile and practical. This book contains material from various sources plus a crystallisation of all that I've learned firsthand, from many years of experience.

Questionnaires, interviews and general correspondence are, in many ways, a natural extension of personal experience as a source of material for the author. Such methods though, are not always appropriate. For example, I could have despatched a questionnaire to other non-fiction authors, seeking information on their work style. But knowing others' preferences wouldn't make me change mine; I doubt if you would change yours. I decided therefore it was not worth a questionnaire survey.

Some aspiring non-fiction authors overlook the less conventional research sources. A lot of detailed research goes into the making of radio and TV documentaries – the wise non-fiction author records and saves relevant programmes for possible future reference. Publicity brochures and advertisements will often provide useful background information for non-specialist non-fiction books. It is always worth retaining odd bits of relevant ephemera too – tickets, programmes, etc – as memory aids if nothing else. (I even have several beer mats in my files with snippets of useful information on their reverse sides.)

Books and magazines

Most non-fiction authors keep themselves up to date with goings-on in at least the part of their field that interests them. Certainly the successful ones do. Usually this entails reading the appropriate specialist journals. Specialist magazines will carry reviews of most of the new books in your field, so you will at least know what you have not yet read.

It is also important not to neglect small news items about your interests in daily papers. Cut them out, mark the source, stick them on sheets of A4 paper and file them carefully.

However, few of us can afford to buy our own copies of all the magazines relevant to all our interests, many of us have to borrow or share others' copies. Were it not for the photocopier, often available in public libraries or in local shops, we would need to make notes of important articles. Photocopies are (relatively) cheap and they should be an important part of every non-fiction author's research 'library'.

A successful non-fiction author is squirrel-like, saving more and more snippets of possibly valuable information. Make sure you save it in an organised and retrievable way though. More on storage and retrieval systems later.

And so we come, as research sources, to books. A non-fiction author should, as far as possible, read all the books in their field. (Set aside your prejudices against marking books. Underline important sections and make marginal explanatory notes in your own books. Marked-up books are easier to extract information from than those in pristine condition. Books are for use.)

With books though, even more than with magazines, few authors can afford to buy them all. Some must be borrowed. It is neither financially practical nor legally permissible to photocopy large chunks of a book, nor is a simple copy or extract what is usually required. Of far more use to the non-fiction author would be a few pages of notes, summarising whole chapters, plus the odd, brief, verbatim extract.

Books by numbers

It's useful to understand a little of how books are classified.

All books published anywhere in the world carry a unique International Standard Book Number (ISBN). From January 2007, the original 10-digit system (ISBN-10) was overtaken by a similar but expanded 13-digit system (ISBN-13, now referred to simply as ISBN). The non-fiction author will find an understanding of the ISBN system useful.

The ISBN-10 system had four distinct, but variable-sized, sections, representing, in order:

■ The country code. (For example, 0 and 1 for English-speaking countries, 2 for French-speaking, and so on.)

'A successful non-fiction author is squirrel-like, saving more and more snippets of possibly valuable information.'

- The publisher prefix. (For example, HarperCollins is 00 and 01, Penguin is 14 and Need2Know is 86144. A small self-publisher would usually be allocated a seven-digit publisher prefix.)

- The title identifier. (A number unique to each book. Publishers are allocated a block of numbers of sufficient digits to retain, with the check digit, the overall 10-digit consistency.)

- The check digit (A single number which, read with the other digits, 'proves' the correctness of the whole ISBN.)

To illustrate, the previous edition of this book had the 10-digit ISBN:

1	–	902713	–	02	–	8
English-speaking country		Writers' Bookshop		How To Write Non-Fiction Books		Check

The 13-digit ISBN follows the same pattern as the 10-digit one but has an 'article number' (the EAN identifies consumer goods, in this case books which is number 978) added in front. Because of the additional digits, the check number will differ from any earlier 10-digit ISBN.

Thus, this revised, retitled, updated and republished edition of this book has a new ISBN:

978	–	1	–	86144	–	114	–	0
Book		English-speaking country		Need2Know Books		Writing Non-Fiction Books		Check

To locate a book in your library, it helps to understand the Dewey Decimal classification system as used by most British libraries.

The Dewey system classifies books under 10 main headings, numbered from 000 by hundreds to 900, which can be subdivided again and again, using as many as six or seven digits, and separated where necessary by decimal points. The main classes and some sample subdivisions are:

000 General works
100 Philosophy
200 Religion
300 Social sciences
400 Languages
500 Pure science
600 Technology   –   610 Medicine
                           620 Engineering   –   621 Mechanical
                           630 Agriculture   622 Mining
                                                      623 Military

700 Fine arts
800 Literature
900 History

Under Dewey, biographies are separately shelved and arranged alphabetically under the surname of the subject-person.

The Internet

For years now, computer prices have been tumbling as fast as their performance has improved. The Internet is now available, with a Broadband connection, to virtually every household in Britain. The world and his wife have linked up. It's simple.

Linking one's PC to the Internet needs no more than a modem (to convert text into material that can pass down the telephone lines), a service provider (ISP) to enable you access and a network browser (often 'bundled' with the computer's operating system). Getting connected is not a difficult task – the programs 'hold your hand' and guide you through the registration processes.

Once connected, you can use the web to send and receive email (electronic mail) from any number of people, worldwide, and your browser (a program) will let you 'surf the net' – explore the worldwide web of available information.

This is not a computer book. You'll find no specialist technical advice here. But a few suggestions:

■ To obtain encyclopaedic (and more) type information, you should search.

For this you need to use a search engine. There are many such, some better than others, and it pays to identify the search engines that best meet your writing needs. The best known and most people's automatic choice is Google (www.google.com). And over time you are bound to encounter Wikipedia (www.wikipedia.org), which is not a search engine but an online encyclopedia.

A small warning though, sometimes information online is not wholly accurate. You may find a website that is supplied by a school class and they sometimes get things wrong, although usually the teacher picks this up and amends it. Equally, some comments are bigoted or biased. It is wise to double-check all information. With regards to Wikipedia, it is also worth noting that as it's a collaborative website and anyone can edit it, so it might not be 100% accurate.

- If you ask a search engine to find you information on say, Alexander Bell, you will get a list of web pages (called 'hits') containing both names. By default, most search engines return only pages that include all your search terms (aside from very common words such as 'it' and 'how', which appear in so many places they won't improve your results), so you don't need to add in 'and'.

- To search for a name or phrase exactly as you have typed it without change, enclose it in double quote marks. However, this can lead to missing relevant pages. For example, a search for "Alexander Bell" will miss pages that refer to Alexander G Bell.

- To exclude terms, attach a minus sign directly in front of the words you wish to exclude. For example, Sussex castles -Arundel will bring up all pages about Sussex castles with no mention of Arundel. You can exclude as many terms as you like.

- If you're interested in alternatives, use OR in capital letters. Dogs poodles OR labradors will bring up pages with either poodles or labradors mentioned, not just those with both.

Some functions vary from search engine to search engine, but most will have a help page with tips for refining your search.

- To find an expert with whom you might be able to discuss a subject, you can avail yourself of one of the many news/discussion groups. Using relevant keywords, search for an appropriate forum. Once found, explain who you are and what you want and post a request for anyone with the expertise you want to contact you. (Note: it is considered impolite to leave messages in capital letters – stick to lower case.) With just a little luck, you'll soon be interviewing an expert by email.

- Newsgroups in your specialist subject(s) may be worth joining in on regularly.

The one big disadvantage of the Internet is that it can become addictive and thus both time-consuming and expensive. You must always remember that you are a writer, seeking information for your writing. If you spend too long surfing the net or chatting cheerfully, you'll never get your book finished. Beware!

Note taking

Nothing is more valuable to non-fiction authors than their own personal notes. A writer's needs will differ from those of a non-writer.

A prime essential in any writer's note is the source. The full title of a book and the author's name or details of the website should be the first things to note down. It is both common sense and common courtesy to be able to cite the source when challenged. A writer also needs to record the publisher's name and the copyright date and edition.

It is also worth recording details of where a book was borrowed from. If the book was borrowed from or consulted at a library, it is helpful to record the ISBN, the Dewey classification and at which library the book is kept. (Some special interest books may not be available from your local library; they can be specially borrowed for you from any library in the country. If you can tell your friendly local librarian where the book was previously borrowed from, it should expedite re-borrowing.) If the book was borrowed from a friend or contact, or, as perhaps when researching a biography, consulted in a family library, it will be helpful to record details. You may need to re-consult.

Depending on the type of research, the notes themselves might be brief summaries of each chapter or merely notes of particular points of interest. Sometimes you will wish to quote verbatim; at other times you will merely wish to make an aide memoire. (But beware: after several years, most memoires

'Nothing is more valuable to non-fiction authors than their own personal notes.'

need a lot of aide-ing! Fuller notes usually repay the extra time they take.) It is, of course, essential that all notes are correct and accurate; inaccuracy can be disastrous.

Whatever type of notes you make, make them on A4 paper (see filing advice, opposite) and leave plenty of space around them. Cramped notes are almost worthless. In later years, they may not even be readable. Blank space on a page not only makes the notes look easier to read, it also provides space for later annotation.

For notes made on a laptop computer, leave an extra-wide margin and always print them out. A hard copy is essential, no matter how much you love your computer. Plenty of signpost-headings and tabulations are also helpful in rereading your notes.

I recommend including the page number of the source. This speeds up relocating a reference – because when you need to check, time is always short.

With some technical subjects, diagrams are often an effective summary of part of the text. Always photocopy (or, if on the web, download) such summary diagrams, even if otherwise you're only making notes from the book or site.

Of course, books are not the only source of a non-fiction author's notes. With story-line type books, the non-fiction author will often wish to interview someone. Few people nowadays will object to an interviewer using a portable recorder. If the subject does object, or clams up when confronted by the recorder, you must rely on making quick, brief, handwritten notes. Recorded or not, write up the notes or transcribe the recording as soon as possible after the interview while it is all fresh in your memory.

Record too (on paper), your personal impressions of all sorts of things: from holiday atmosphere to an interviewee's home and furnishings, from instructional anecdote material to the state of repair of specific historic buildings.

Filing systems

The research for a book can take a long time. In order to become an expert in your field, you have inevitably gone through a lengthy learning process. It would have been helpful if you had read this chapter before you started. That impossibility apart, let's consider organisation.

Your researches will, over time, result in a vast amount of information on sheets of paper. This collection of information is fine. A pile of papers in a box under the bed is of little use though; information has to be organised. The 'ordinary interested reader' may not need to be systematic, but the writer does. The non-fiction author must be able to retrieve information when it's needed.

A good first step is to ensure that all notes are on A4 pages that are double-hole punched for filing. Paste small cuttings onto hole-punched sheets and punch holes in photocopies and pages torn from magazines. File them all. There is nothing sacrosanct about the A4 size, but most photocopies, many magazines and most typing and writing paper are all A4, so why not standardise on it?

A good way of filing your A4 sheets safely is in big lever-arch files. But you need to be able to retrieve all the information you've got on specific aspects of your subject(s) quickly and easily.

One way of organising the files is to letter each file and number each sheet therein, as inserted. Each sheet in the file can be listed on contents sheets at the front of the file. But you still need to find which sheets relate to which aspect of the subject. For that, a separate card index will help.

Sheet B256 might be a photocopy of an article titled 'Dragons in Chinese Art'. In the card index there will already be cards labelled: Dragons – general, Dragons – Chinese, Monsters, Chinese mythology, British folklore, etc. On both the 'Dragons – Chinese' and 'Chinese mythology' cards, add a line:

Article, Dragons in Chinese Art (The Lady 26Jan99) – B256

With such cards it is easy to locate and extract the relevant papers for easy reference.

This block filing and card index referencing system is logical, effective and flexible. I commend it to anyone just starting. It is not though, the system I use.

'You need to be able to retrieve all the information you've got on specific aspects of your subject quickly and easily.'

My own system is looser, much less tidy, and... just grew. As above, it is based on A4 sheets, but the filing system is simpler. I have a clear plastic sleeve for each aspect of each subject I am interested in. Related sleeves are kept together in card wallet-files that are then stored in a filing cabinet. As a photocopy or page of notes is prepared, it is simply stuffed into the relevant sleeve. Once a sleeve or file becomes too fat, I subdivide it. With this system, I can quickly review what I have on any subject. But my cross-referencing is undoubtedly less than 100% effective.

This system is less well organised than the card index method recommended above, but I am more interested in writing than in filing. Develop your filing and retrieval system. It doesn't matter what system, as long as it works. Your objective is to know your subject, not to have the world's best filing system.

Summing Up

■ You need to know your subject thoroughly (subject to any self-imposed limitations in scope or readership). Make sure you have all the necessary information at your fingertips.

■ There is no copyright in facts, but there is in the way the facts are presented. Don't copy others' work: learn from it.

■ Research your subject fully. Sources include personal experience and observation, original research in the form of questionnaires, interviews, published material and the Internet.

■ Make notes of where your information is taken from. It helps to record a reference source's International Standard Book Number (ISBN) and/or its library classification (the Dewey system).

■ Don't rely on your memory. Make notes of your research and file them carefully and systematically.

Chapter Three

Developing the Idea

The non-fiction author must be a salesperson; they must get out and sell each new book idea. (Agents are seldom the answer for a non-fiction author; the big money's usually in fiction or 'big names' and that's where the agents operate.) To sell, the book itself must be accurately aimed at a market to which, in turn, the publisher can sell.

So far in our professional approach to non-fiction authorship, we have thought of an idea for a book and started researching its content. It is still not yet time to start writing the book. We have to sell it first.

The sales package

To sell our book to a publisher, we have to have something concrete to sell – what I call a sales package. We have to persuade a publisher to buy our idea for a book. To do this, we have to show that we have thought the idea through and that it has the makings of an attractive book with good sales potential.

The non-fiction author's sales package should consist of:

- A description of the target reader.
- An assessment of the market for the book.
- The author's credentials: why you are the ideal person to write the book.

And, separately:

- A detailed description of the book: a chapter by chapter synopsis and a good title.

'We have to show that we have thought the idea through and that it has the makings of an attractive book with good sales potential.'

The first three items – readership, market and credentials – can sensibly be run together: a covering proposal introducing the synopsis to follow. Together, the proposal and the synopsis form the sales package.

The target reader

Your concept of the target reader is a major factor in writing a successful non-fiction book. The potential reader has to feel at ease with the way a book is written.

It is in the attitude to the reader that the successful writer differs most sharply from the beginner. The beginner writes what they want to write to please him/herself. The successful writer supplies what the reader wants.

To write at just the right level and in just the right tone for the reader means accurately identifying that reader. In writing, describe your target reader in as much detail as possible.

This may entail identifying, for a management text say, such details as typical job title, functions, responsibilities and age; for a children's textbook, the year and grade at what type of school, perhaps. In other cases, the reader may be described merely as a keen walker, interested in nature and knowing what to look out for under hedge bottoms.

Identify too, the reader's prime need. In planning this book, I identified your need as to know:

- How to organise, structure and communicate your thoughts, knowledge and experience.

- How best to sell your ideas and eventually present your work to achieve acceptance for publication.

Those needs are constantly in my mind while I'm writing this book.

When identifying and describing your target reader, don't think only about this country. Consider the possibility that there might be a much larger market – the whole English-speaking world perhaps. (Don't get too carried away though, a guidebook to pubs in the South of England is unlikely to sell many copies in Quebec or Singapore – nor even in Liverpool or Glasgow.) If appropriate, you must then bear in mind the needs of the overseas reader, which will differ in level, perhaps. Different things may need to be made clear. Lack of clarity is, for a non-fiction author, a major failing.

One way of coping with the problems of differing levels of understanding is to add either basic explanation or more complicated material 'off line'. This can be in illustrations, appendices or what article writers call 'sidebars'. (A sidebar is a self-contained, boxed-in supplement to a feature article otherwise complete in itself.) Look at present-day children's encyclopaedias, etc, for the effective use of boxed-in 'bites', often called 'factfiles' or similar, of extra information. Check with your publisher before adopting this approach though – it is not appropriate in all types of book.

Don't add extra explanation in the form of footnotes. Footnotes are old-fashioned and academic. They make the typesetter's life more difficult, which means the price goes up, and they look unattractive.

Think 'book'

After the determination of the target reader, the content and size of the book is the next most important of the initial 'building blocks'. The non-fiction author must think book. Basically, a book has to be… book sized. But that's too vague to be helpful.

Some 'how to' books are no more than 30,000 words long. (This book is about that length.) Most other non-fiction books are longer. There is virtually no maximum limit – but the longer a non-fiction book is, the more expensive to produce, therefore the higher the list price and the harder to sell.

Let's think about an average non-fiction book containing about 40,000 words. (There's nothing rigid about that figure, it's just useful as a basis for what follows.)

Such a non-fiction book might well be divided into eight to 12 chapters, averaging about 4,000-5,000 words per chapter. Shorter-than-average chapters are usually a sign of bad planning. They suggest that the author doesn't know much about those aspects of the subject. Conversely, extra-long chapters make a book look difficult (and it's certainly hard to find one's way around in such books). Let's say 10 chapters at 4,000 words.

The synopsis

The purpose of the synopsis is threefold:

- To demonstrate to a publisher that you will cover the subject adequately. (He may wish to suggest further aspects to be covered, which can be helpful to the author.)

- To act as the first checklist of material to be covered by the author when actually writing.

- To give a general feel of the proposed book's contents for the publisher's sales team and, through them, for potential customers.

The synopsis has to show, in detail, chapter by chapter, the content of your book and it must do so in a logical, understandable way. A warning though: do not become too firmly committed to your synopsis. This is for two reasons.

First, the publisher who accepts your sales package may wish to vary its content or sequence. It is usually wise to go along with such suggestions, as they will be intended to improve the book and its sales potential. Besides, the publisher is the paymaster, or will be.

The second reason for synopsis-flexibility is that, as the book develops, you will find that you wish to make changes yourself. You may find some new or essential aspect that both you and your publisher have overlooked. You must take this on board. Absorb it into your synopsis plan, though remember to keep the publisher in the picture. Don't surprise him on delivery.

At the end of your synopsis, say roughly how long, in round thousands of words, you expect the book to be and whether and to what extent it will be illustrated.

I have already explained that I classify non-fiction books as either technical or story-line. The form in which the synopsis is prepared will vary between the two book types. First, the synopsis for the technical book.

The technical synopsis

List as many separate parts of your subject as you can. These are potential chapters. At this stage, don't worry about logic or sequence, concentrate on dividing the whole into self-contained parts and on ensuring that you really have covered it all. Every subject can be subdivided. If you have not already done so, now is the time to do it.

My initial thoughts about this book were, in random order:

- Attitude of mind – professionalism (don't write until the idea is sold).
- The basic idea – who will read it? (The target reader).
- Selling the idea – approaching publishers (there are lots – how to choose).
- Production and publicity – help the publisher to sell your book.
- Business matters – royalties, agreements, tax.
- Organising content, structure and writing.
- Writing equipment.
- The writing process – write to budget, accuracy, brevity, clarity.
- Illustrations.
- Preparing the typescript.
- The index – when and how.
- Editing – commissioning and copy editors.
- Proofs and proofreading.
- Next book – and/or revised edition(s).
- Writer's library.
- Research techniques.

That's too many self-contained parts. I don't want more than about 10 to make 10 chapters. (Remember?) Perhaps some can be rethought and run together?

The next stages – and they tend to run together – are to rearrange the chapter ideas into a logical sequence and to expand on the contents of each chapter. There is seldom just one single correct sequence, merely different people's opinions. (For example, for this book some might use a sequence based on: content – writing – selling. I believe that selling should come earlier on. My preferred sequence is: idea – content – selling – writing.) In order to understand one chapter, it is important to ensure that the reader doesn't have to read a later chapter to make sense of it. This is not as easy as it sounds, for many techniques need a repetitive process.

I made several changes to my initial thoughts. I wanted to expound my overall '10 steps' professional approach early on in the book. I also needed to explain my grouping of the variety of non-fiction books into just two broad types.

The answer was an introduction, which is often a good idea to indicate how the book will deal with the subject. There was no question that I had to bring research right forward – that was clearly in completely the wrong place. And several other 'bits' could indeed, with advantage, be run together.

Compare my initial list with the contents page. I think the end result makes good sense.

Having decided on the chapters and their sequence, you need to think about the content of individual chapters. This is effectively the same process as before, but within a more limited scope. You know what you meant by your initial headings, now expand on them. These chapter expansions should be fairly brief, yet make it clear that you will cover the content adequately.

To illustrate the coverage of a synopsis, the details given for this chapter were:

Developing the Idea: The components of the essential sales package to offer to publishers. Defining the target reader. 'Think book', say 10 chapters, each 4,000 words. Alternative types of synopsis. 'Selling' titles. The proposal.

(This chapter does not follow the synopsis exactly, its organisation was refined during the actual writing process – see chapter 5.)

You may feel that there are some separate but small aspects of your subject that don't justify a chapter to themselves. In technical books, one solution is to include, at the end, a miscellany chapter. Another method, of course, is to bend your chapter subjects to accommodate extra material. Or you can add appendices at the end of the book.

The story-line synopsis

The synopsis for a story-line type of non-fiction book needs a rather different treatment. The writing may be approached much like a novel, but the selling process requires the non-fiction sales package proposal and synopsis.

First though, the story-line non-fiction author, like the technical author, has to think all around the subject. Again, list all aspects of the subject: the subject-person's life (or that portion to be covered), the battle or complete war, the sporting occasion, the country (or the author's own travels). Then ponder on first their completeness, and then the best chapter order in which to include them. Should you start with the reasons for the war, the history of the race, the statistics of the country or should you start with a bang?

If you are proposing to write a biography (the story of someone's life) or the story of a battle, war, sporting event, etc, it's often good to start with what fiction writers call a hook. This is something really gripping that will immediately interest the potential reader; a turning point in the story. This is an approach well fitted to the light, popular type of biography/autobiography – the type most akin to fiction – recording only a small part of the subject's whole life span. The more serious, 'heavier' biographies tend to be written in full chronological sequence.

The synopsis for a story-line type of non-fiction book must show whether the sequence is to be chronological or whether it will include flashbacks. (The flashback is another fictional technique where early back-story is introduced out of sequence to explain some action or attitude.)

One of these days, I shall get round to writing a biography of Sylvia Pankhurst. (Any publishers interested?) She was *Not Just a Suffragette* (my potential title). She was also an artist, a poet, a journalist and non-fiction author and an

'You need to demonstrate to the potential publisher that you will cover the subject sufficiently.'

ardent, before-her-time feminist. She was an early British communist and an Ethiopian 'saint'. My chapter plan for this book runs chronologically but with 'offline' chapters on her writing and other aspects of a fascinating life.

When writing the in-chapter details for a story-line type of non-fiction book, there needs to be just as much description as for the technical book. You need to demonstrate to the potential publisher that you will cover the subject sufficiently. Like this extract from my draft Sylvia Pankhurst synopsis:

7 Sylvia's War (1914-1918): The family turns 'jingo', while Sylvia is pacifist and increasingly socialist. She works hard for 'her' East Enders, opening the 'Penny Carltons', the 'Mother's Arms' (an ex-pub), the toy factory, etc. The League of Rights and her sweated labour campaign. Her enthusiasm at the Russian Revolution; she opens/founds the People's Russian Information Bureau. Her Derby speech. The limited impact of the granting of women's suffrage on Sylvia. The 'coupon' election of 1918.

As with all non-fiction books, the same warning applies – don't get too committed to your synopsis at this stage. Publishers may want to change the coverage or the treatment. You should be as flexible as possible.

End your story-line synopsis with an estimate of the book's planned length and say whether illustrations are proposed.

'The title is most effective if it is brief and catchy.'

The book's title

Another important element of the sales package is a striking title. The purpose of the title is to attract favourable attention, to identify the book and, persuasively, to describe its content. It is most effective if it is brief and catchy.

A title such as *A Manual of Conceptual Design Standards and Policies for Widget Technicians*, which might have been acceptable 100 years ago, would not be so today. It looks old-fashioned; it is too lengthy to be easily referred to; it has no sales impact at all; and it would not fit in as a running head across the pages. The printer would also find it troublesome to print all that on the spine of a slim, 30,000 words book.

You should never be surprised if your publisher – once you and he are committed – wants to change the title of your non-fiction book. Publishers often know, better than the author, what makes a good selling title. But work at developing a good title yourself anyway. Even if later discarded, it will have played its part in selling the idea to the publisher.

Aim at a title of no more than four or five words. Subtitles can supplement a short title, but not all publishers welcome them.

Investigate other books of a similar nature to yours. Notice the use, in technical titles, of such phrases as 'How To…', 'Successful…' and 'Profit from…'. They all suggest that buying the book will benefit the reader. Notice also that technical titles clearly indicate the subject. An allusive or quotation title is sometimes acceptable for the story-line type of non-fiction book but seldom if ever for the technical type book.

The proposal

The other part of the sales package, the proposal, is the 'hard sell' document seeking to persuade the publisher to accept your idea and the accompanying synopsis.

In my view, the proposal should be no more than one sheet of single-spaced typescript. (The synopsis should similarly, I believe, be complete within no more than about two sheets of single-spaced typescript, or the equivalent. I do not recommend double-spaced typing for the proposal and synopsis.)

Firstly, the proposal needs to show who will buy the proposed book – the target readership. Secondly, it needs to show either:

- How the technical book reader will benefit – by greater enjoyment of a hobby or better knowledge of how to do something, by getting a better job or achieving promotion, or by improved chances of exam success.

Or:

- What is so special/interesting/unusual/amusing about the subject of the story-line book? Refresh the publisher's memory about the characteristics of the subject-person, the nature of the sport, the attractions of the country. Mention too, any forthcoming anniversary, event or date to which the book's launch can be linked. (Allow time for the book to be considered, commissioned, written, produced and launched – say three years.) 'Sell' the subject.

Next, for both types of non-fiction book, outline:

- Your qualifications for writing this book – your 'author's credentials'. Avoid false modesty – sell yourself. (But be careful, once sold, you must live up to it.)

- The competition. How your book will differ from, and be better than, other books on the market. Identify the market niche.

- Roughly how long, given a go-ahead, you would require before delivering the book.

Here too, as well as at the end of the synopsis, state:

- The approximate length you propose the book to be – be willing to vary this if required – and whether illustrations are planned.

The example opposite shows how I would put up a proposal – for a mythical book. It all fits on a single sheet of paper.

A checklist for the sales package

When you have completed your sales package, check it out against this list:

- Is the book title short, catchy and descriptive?

- Have you clearly identified the target reader? Have you explained why the reader will want to read your book?

- Have you described the book in the best possible terms? Have you fully covered the subject?

- Have you sold yourself as the ideal person to write the book?

- Does the synopsis clearly show the content of each chapter? Does the synopsis demonstrate that there is the right amount of subject matter?

- Have you compared competitive books and explained how yours will be better?

- Does the book meet the requirements of any relevant examination syllabi?

Widgets are the latest craze! Everyone, it seems, wants their own widget. Nor are widgets likely to be a mere nine-day wonder: there have been British enthusiasts, widget users, since widgets were first introduced to this country in the early 1960s.

There are widget-user clubs all over the country – and with the current enthusiasm, many more clubs are being formed. At the last count – according to the British Association of Widget Users' current yearbook – there were 1,257 registered clubs with a nationwide membership of nearly 20,000 enthusiasts. The new clubs, catering for the current enthusiasm, will boost that number considerably.

The only thing holding back the tide of potential widget users is the initial expense. Widgets are not cheap. But, surprisingly, they are simple to make and the necessary components are relatively inexpensive. Anyone could make their own. If you _Make Your Own Widget_ you will save hundreds of pounds compared with the cost of a 'bought widget'. And a bonus: making your own, you learn how it works.

All 20,000 Association members – and the new recruits even more so – are likely to be interested in making their own widgets. My book will be aimed specifically at the beginners – while offering valuable advice to the 'old hands' too. There would seem to be an excellent potential market for it.

There are several books available about widgets and their use. Most of them are written and published in America – and few American practices translate well into British. The few British-orientated books about widgets are very technical, aimed at the experienced user – the techno-boffin. And while the existing books explain the construction of commercial widgets only one, _Widget Construction_ by Rodney Wager (Grenally Books), goes into details of self-construction. Wager's book, however, is three years old – and developments are rapid in the widget world – and very hard to work from; it is more of an academic book than a 'how to' book.

My book will be simple: readily understandable by the ordinary man-in-the-street with no technical background. It will assume no prior knowledge or experience of widgets. It will show you how to *Make Your Own Widget*. It will therefore be ideal for the burgeoning new market. It will, at present, have little competition.

I am ideally placed to write this book. I have owned and used widgets for more than 10 years; I have made all of them myself, with great success. I know how to do it.

Not only do I know how to make widgets, but for the last four years at one day adult education courses I have been successfully teaching others how to make them.

In addition to my widget experience, I am a competent technical author; I have published three previous books and nearly a 100 general-interest and technical articles. The attached sheet lists my books and a selection of the articles. You can be sure that my book will be well – and competently – written.

As you will see from the enclosed synopsis, I envisage the book as being about 40,000 words long, with many (40+) of my own photographs as illustrations. Given a go-ahead I would expect to be able to deliver the book within four months – hopefully to catch the current wave of enthusiasm.

....

Gordon Wells

(Address, Date, Telephone, etc)

An example of how a proposal might be worded – for a strictly mythical book. Notice the key points: an assessment of the potential market; mention of the competition; what the book will do for the reader; and why the author is the ideal person to provide it. Notice too the enthusiasm.

Summing Up

- To sell the idea of your book to a potential publisher you need a sales package. This should consist of a description of the target reader, your assessment of the market for the book, your credentials for writing the book, and, separately, a chapter by chapter synopsis of the book – and a really good title.

- Break up your book content into chapters, each covering a specific part of the subject. As a preliminary guide, think in terms of about 10 chapters, each of maybe 4,000-5,000 words each. Avoid occasional extra-long or extra-short chapters.

- Broadly speaking, there are two types of synopsis: the technical and the story-line. Both types must demonstrate to the publisher that you will cover the subject fully, to act as a checklist of coverage and to give a general feel of the book's content.

- A good title is of great importance. Keep it short (say five words maximum), positive and self-explanatory.

Chapter Four

Selling the idea

The sales package complete, you now have something concrete to sell. (And again, remember: a non-fiction book should usually be 'sold' before it is written.)

Not all publishers will be interested in the type of book you propose. Your first task is to list all those who might be interested, and then from that list, persuade one to publish it. A good place to start reviewing potential publishers is to see who has published other books on the same general subject. If your book is not in direct competition with one of their existing books, they may be interested.

Researching publishers

List the publishers of books on the same or similar subjects on your own shelves. Extend this list by looking in bookshops and libraries. With the more technical book subjects, the resultant list will seldom be long. With story-line type books, you will probably need to look more carefully: many publishers publish biographies and so-called 'general non-fiction' – you will need to investigate further the areas and 'weight' of such books. (There is a major difference between a biography of popstar Hubert Pumpernickel and one of the late, great King Cedricson of Ruritania; the publisher of one will often not consider the other.)

Don't overlook the smaller, specialist publishers; not every good book is published by the giants. Conversely, don't shy completely away from the major publishing houses; they are just as keen to publish good non-fiction books as are the smaller publishers. (Unfortunately though, some bigger publishers are increasingly unwilling to consider proposals other than through literary agents. See chapter 9.)

'Your first task is to list all those who might be interested, and then from that list, persuade one to publish it.'

There are several annual reference books that are useful for researching possible publishers. *The Writers' and Artists' Yearbook* (A&C Black) and *The Writer's Handbook* (Macmillan) are both well established but tend to include only the larger, better-known publishers (and many overseas ones too).

It is also very helpful to consult each year's two special issues of *The Bookseller* magazine: the spring and autumn issues. Your local librarian almost certainly gets copies – check in the library's reference section. These two thick volumes list virtually every new book being published in the UK in the following six months, classified by subject areas. There are also advertisements of forthcoming books by most of the major publishers. The monthly, subscription only, *Writers' News* (see help list for details) is also a particularly good source of information about lesser-known or new publishers.

Once you have identified a number of potential publishers for your proposed book, it's worth studying the catalogues of your possible front runners. Most publishers will send you their current catalogue if you phone and ask. And you can of course, once identified, look at the publishers' pages on the Internet.

The catalogues will tell you a lot about the publisher's books in the same general area as yours. You may be able to discern an underlying pattern in their books that might preclude or encourage yours. Look particularly for existing book series into which yours – perhaps amended – could fit. Fitting your book into an existing series will please the publisher, who will wish the series to expand regularly, and be better for you, the author. Series of books tend to encourage serial sales.

From all your market research, sort your list into order. At the top of the list should be the publisher you judge most likely to be interested in your book. (This won't necessarily be the major publisher you'd most like to be published by.)

Approaching publishers

You are now ready to write to your first-choice publisher. Yes, even if you live just around the corner from his office, write to him. Submit your sales package (as described in the previous chapter) plus covering letter by post, or you could email a slightly more tentative enquiry to the publisher along the lines of 'Would you be willing to look at details of a proposed new non-fiction book about…?'

Your letter, and the sales package, will of course be typed. (More on presentation in chapter 7.) Anything handwritten will barely get a cursory glance before certain rejection.

The covering letter accompanying the sales package can be brief; everything important is in the sales package. When approaching a new-to-me publisher with a book idea, I say something like:

Dear Mr Bloggs

I am writing to enquire whether you might be interested in a new book about [Subject]. My working title is [Title]. I believe it will fit snugly into your '[Series Title]' series.

I enclose a brief note about the book, including an assessment of the possible market for it, the competing books and my own credentials for writing it, together with a detailed synopsis.

Should you wish to see sample chapters, chapters 2 and 3 are virtually complete; I could let you have these within days of an expression of interest.

I enclose a stamped addressed envelope for your reply.

Yours sincerely

Gordon Wells

- Address someone at the publisher's office by name. Unless you already have the name of a contact person, telephone the firm and ask the operator for the name of the editorial director.

- It's better that you specify the chapters you have ready (even if they aren't quite finished). That way, you can choose those aspects on which you are most up to speed. If not, the publisher may ask to see specific chapters which, this early on, you may be less ready to write.

- Provision of the stamped addressed envelope makes it more likely that you will get a reply. Most, but sadly not all, publishers are polite enough to do that. No SAE makes a reply much less likely.

Multiple submissions

'If making multiple submissions, let the publishers know.'

If you believe that there are a number of suitable publishers who might be interested in your book idea, then multiple submission may be the right approach. This practice is now widely adopted and, grudgingly, accepted. The author doesn't have to wait two or three months again and again as one publisher after another rejects a marginal idea. (Really rotten ideas usually get a quicker brush-off.) But it is important that each of the publishers to whom you simultaneously submit your sales package is aware that others are also considering it.

It is debatable whether or not you should divulge the names of the several considering publishers. Certainly, as soon as one of the publishers makes an acceptable offer to publish your book, you should notify the other publishing houses and withdraw it from offer. (Unless everyone knows it's an auction, but that's an unknown world for most non-fiction authors.)

Personally, I have not yet found it necessary or desirable to make multiple submission offers to publishers; most of my books are of relatively narrow interest. Multiple submissions are a matter of individual circumstances and personal decision.

Once the letters and sales packages have been despatched, for both multiple and single submissions, forget them as best you can. Don't expect a speedy reply. After a month, you could try a delicate reminder, 'enquiring whether there is any news'. You might follow this up with a courteous telephone enquiry.

If you haven't heard within two or three months, you have to decide whether to send a further reminder or withdraw the idea from offer to that publisher. A long delay might mean that several people are reading and seriously considering your idea, or it could equally mean that there is a large backlog of unsolicited material and a 'snowed-under' reader.

It's often best just to sit it out with occasional reminders. Meanwhile, get on with something else.

Rejection

Prepare yourself. Your sales package may be rejected. Don't be too upset by this. I doubt whether there is a non-fiction author around who hasn't had book ideas rejected by the first publisher approached.

When you get a rejection letter, curse, take a deep breath and resubmit a new copy of the sales package to the second of your preferred publishers. If he rejects it, resubmit to number three, and so on. Apart from helping you to survive the rejection pains, resubmission keeps the idea out 'on offer'.

If you get several rapid rejections though, stop and think. Did any give their reasons? If so, is there a common theme? Think about it. Otherwise, possible reasons for rejection include:

- The idea is lousy.

- There is no market for the idea.

- The package does not present the idea well.

- All the publishers really are over-stocked for their future programmes – unlikely, except in a recession.

- There are already enough books on the market on the subject. Did you fall down in your market research?

- You are trying the wrong publishers. Again, is your market research at fault?

Assuming that after your rethink you remain convinced that the idea is worth proceeding with, that there is a market for it and that the sales package presents the idea as well as possible, off you go again. Although most publishers are astute judges of books, they can – and do – make mistakes.

(Don't be put off if you hear that a book on the same subject is being prepared by another author. It is unlikely that both will cover exactly the same ground.) Submit the sales package to the next publisher on the list.

If I were convinced that my idea was good, I would not give up until I'd been rejected maybe 15-20 times. (And possibly not even then, if I could still see some likely publishers.)

But let's be more optimistic. One of your high-listed preferred publishers shows interest. You might get a phone call asking you to come and discuss the project. More likely, you will receive a letter asking to see some sample chapters and, ideally, agreeing to look at the ones you've mentioned. The publisher needs the sample chapters to assure himself that you know how to write: you may have put together an excellent synopsis and proposal but turn out not to be much good at explaining, teaching or story telling.

Sample chapters

'The sample chapters must be the very best you are capable of.'

The sample chapters must be the very best you are capable of. They are your samples. A lot will hang on how they impress the publisher: their clarity, their easy readability and their coverage.

They must be complete in every respect: if the finished book is to have illustrations, worked examples and exercises, then so must the samples. And don't keep the publisher waiting too long for them. You want to get back to him while he's still interested and enthusiastic. Don't give him time to forget you and your interesting idea; there's always another interesting book idea about to land on his desk.

There will be detailed advice on the organisation, mechanics and process of writing and presenting non-fiction in the next few chapters. You need to take all of this advice on board when preparing your samples.

Unless the publisher tells you otherwise (i.e. to submit by email), post the sample chapters addressed by name to the person you are dealing with. Enclose a stamped addressed envelope in case they wish to return the chapters (but this will often be returned unused). Also enclose a further, small, stamped self-addressed envelope and ask for an acknowledgement of receipt.

You should get an acknowledgement fairly quickly – within a week or so. Don't expect a final decision on the sample chapters that quickly though. The editor will be dealing with a number of book projects, all at different stages and all at the same time. She will read the samples as soon as she can. The editor will not be the only person to read them, either. It's most likely that the samples, together with your initial sales package, will also be sent to one or more readers – possibly experts on the subject of your book – for comments. The readers' comments are not the sole decisive factor on whether or not your book goes ahead, but they are undoubtedly important.

Let's assume that the comments are favourable. The editor will probably decide that she would now like to meet you, for a general and wide-ranging discussion of your book. (If there is not much to discuss, this initial discussion may just be on the phone.) However you 'meet', you're close to a firm acceptance now.

Meeting the publisher

The editor that you now meet will be what is sometimes called the commissioning editor. In smaller publishing houses, the editor may be the only editor you will deal with throughout. At this initial stage, she is operating as a commissioning editor; later she may act as a copy editor (see chapter 8).

The commissioning editor must be enthusiastic about your book; she may have to make the case for it at an editorial board. Once committed, she will be closely involved throughout your book's publication process.

You should be able to lean on her for advice. A good editor/author relationship can blossom into a real friendship.

At this first meeting, the editor may offer suggestions for improving the synopsis: extend the scope here, add in a chapter about this, why not run those two thin chapters together. She may want the whole book to be longer or even shorter. Whatever the suggestions, consider them carefully. Discuss the reasons for them and be prepared to accommodate them or explain why not. The editor sees many more books, across a far wider field, than any author, and will have a better idea of market needs and saleability. She may not know much about your specialist subject, but she will certainly know more than you about publishing.

At your initial meeting, as well as the book's content and framework, you will probably also discuss such important details as overall length, delivery date and the financial and contractual terms that will be offered.

I always make quick, rough notes at such meetings and follow up with a written confirmation of my understanding, as soon as possible, usually by email. All you need now is the go-ahead – the agreement.

Commissioning the book

Unless the commissioning editor has been able to give you the go-ahead at your meeting, which at a small publishing house is possible but at a larger one it's unlikely, you must now wait a little longer. An added advantage of writing to confirm what was agreed at your meeting is that you may thereby provoke a reply advising you that 'an agreement is being prepared'. Given such an exchange, I would start work without waiting for the agreement.

The agreement and associated matters – advances, royalties, etc – are further examined in chapter 9.

Once the agreement is signed by both you and the publisher, you must get down to work in earnest on your book. You are (both) committed. You are committed to a pre-agreed delivery date. Perhaps more important, you are committed to a finished length which will also be pre-agreed.

The publisher prepares his publishing programme many months in advance; he will arrange production schedules, copy-editing, typesetting, printing and binding and publicity all along the line. If the author delivers late, the production schedule is upset, the publisher incurs extra costs and publication is delayed. If the author delivers a short or over-long book, this can upset the whole costing basis on which the book was accepted.

You must work to time and to length. Advice on this is included in the next chapter.

What if the book is 'sold' to you?

Sometimes, particularly for technical books, a publisher himself decides that there is a need for a particular book and goes looking for a suitable person to write it. If you are a recognised expert in some field, this could be you.

A similar situation can arise in the field of children's non-fiction. Most children's publishers have lists of experienced children's authors. The editorial staff come up with an idea for a book and ask one of their preferred authors to work on it for them. What do you do?

The commissioned author is in much the same position as the author with an idea to sell but with much of the uncertainty removed. The publisher wants a book on the subject and wants you to write it. All you have to do is justify the publisher's need and faith.

You still need to do much of what has already been described. Specifically you should:

- Investigate competing texts to see how they have handled the subject.
- Think about how you are going to structure and write the book.
- Assure yourself and the publisher that you can cover the whole subject.
- Prepare the synopsis and obtain editorial agreement.

And maybe…

- Write sample chapters. (If you have not previously worked for the publisher before, he will need assurance of your writing skills.)

From here on, everything in this book applies equally to the author who seeks out the publisher and to the author approached by the publisher. No matter from which side you approach the writing grindstone, your nose will be in the same extended contact with it.

Summing Up

- Identify potential publishers for your book – it's useless offering, for example, a 'how to' book to a publisher who only ever publishes story-line books (or worse, only fiction). Don't overlook the smaller publishers. Study your potential publishers' lists – maybe they have an existing series into which your book could be slotted.

- Preferably, approach your publishers one at a time. If you decide to submit to several simultaneously, let them know (though not necessarily revealing names) right from the start. If one publisher then expresses interest, let the others know to save them wasted effort.

- Write to a named person in the publisher's office, enclosing your sales package and a reply envelope. Don't chase the publisher for a reply in less than a month. Ideally, have a couple of sample chapters ready for delivery and tell the publisher which ones they are (to avoid him asking for ones not yet written).

- If a publisher is interested, they may want changes in the format, reader-level, approach or content. Be flexible and accommodate these changes as much as possible.

- Once accepted, you and the publisher will sign an agreement specifying length, delivery schedule, method and payment arrangements.

Chapter Five

Organising the Book

The book idea is sold, now you have to produce it. Before offering advice on the actual writing, let's consider the organisation of it.

We have already produced the broad overall synopsis for the book. Now is the time to arrange the within-chapter contents in the best, most logical sequence. The logical structure of book and chapter enables the reader to understand and enjoy it.

Organisation is an essential part of the non-fiction author's job.

Organising the chapter content

By organising our book in more-or-less self-contained chapters, we make the task of writing the book more manageable; we are bringing everything down to an understandable scale. We need only think about one chapter at a time – a mere few thousand words.

Let's make the task seem even simpler. We do this by looking in more detail at each chapter's proposed content, considering each of the topics to be covered and in what order. For the chapter you are now reading, my original (overall) synopsis was:

The Mechanics of Writing. Expanding the synopsis into chapter skeletons. Developing within-chapter logic. Counting words ('Writer is someone who counts words.' Braine). Working to a word budget – leading to agreed book length. Importance of a hierarchy of headings. How many drafts? Regularity – writing routine. Illustrations – link with text. Writers' equipment.

It's all there, but it's useful to expand it somewhat before actually writing. And the organisation – the logical sequence – needs to be carefully reviewed.

Even though nowadays I do all my work on a word processor, I still find it easiest to do my book and chapter planning in longhand on paper. I write out the synopsis subjects in a list spread down an A4 page, leaving plenty of space around them. I then expand on the headings, noting the further points I want to make. The points seldom come to me in order – there are always afterthoughts and many changes of mind.

While thinking about the points to include, I also review the logic of their order. Should I start with the word budget or with the structure? Should I mention the need for regular writing before or after I suggest the equipment that might be needed? Do the comments on illustrations belong in this chapter? Arrows criss-cross the page and notes to myself abound. Maybe I come up with an idea for the opening paragraph, which is always important. That's scribbled down on the page too, so that I don't forget it.

'Section headings help the reader find the way around.'

There are computer programs that will help you organise the content of a book or chapter. If you are happy working that way, fine. You'll end up with much the same result as I get from my on-page doodles. (I see little point in using special programs anyway – you can insert and move phrases around with any word processor program, which is all that's needed.)

It's also a good idea to note the target wordage for each section within the chapter. Not only does this let you check on the length but also on the balance – whether you're writing too much about one topic or not enough on another.

Organising the structure

In the technical type of non-fiction book, it helps if the organisation of the book and chapter structure is clear to the reader. Section headings help the reader find the way around. They help in relocating a particular section and they warn of what's ahead. To this end, the hierarchy of headings must be clear and maintained.

Changes in the heading hierarchy are distracting and confusing. Such unwanted changes occur when a chapter starts with simple, one-stage headings (for example, lower-case characters aligned to the left margin) and then, after a page or two, descend to a second stage (centred capitals) and then continues using the second-stage headings throughout the rest of the chapter.

The reader is left wondering whether all the later headings are subsidiary to the last of the early first-stage ones or not. (Usually, the first two or three second-level headings are correctly second level, then the author forgets the original hierarchy and the rest of the headings should have been first-level ones.) Inconsistency in maintaining a hierarchy of headings only demonstrates an author's inability to organise their thoughts and writing.

A non-fiction author should be able to manage (and this only in the more technical of books) with chapter titles and two further levels of heading. (In most non-fiction books, a single level of within-chapter headings should suffice as in this book.)

Headings, both chapter titles and within-chapter headings, should be kept fairly short; seldom more than half a dozen words. The main chapter titles are often used as running heads: page headings. (The book title is usually on the left-hand page, the chapter title on the right.) It doesn't look good if the running heads spread right across the page. The shorter the heading, the more blank space around it, and the more it stands out on the page. It's a more useful signpost.

The more within-chapter headings you use, the more the book pages are split up, the easier to read and more understandable the book appears. Use frequent headings in introductory, popular, 'how to' books and less frequently in heavier tomes. I usually aim to have at least one heading on each double-page spread of the finished book (i.e. a maximum of about a thousand words apart). They are more frequent in this book.

I recommend that you avoid starting a chapter with a heading as it moves the text-proper too low down and it looks awkward. I suggest at least one or two introductory paragraphs before a first heading.

Organising the output

Of equal importance to the organisation and subdivision of chapter content is the length of each section and chapter. You are committed to a book of an agreed length.

As the novelist John Braine says, 'A writer is a person who counts words'. Unless you count your words, you don't know how your output compares with the total requirement. The word count also enables you to keep tags on the topic balance. (I believe that counting your words leads to an improved writing style too – see chapter 6.)

In my view, the best way of keeping a check on the overall book length while maintaining the between- and within-chapter balance is to establish a word budget.

Make a table showing each chapter, appendix, etc and its planned length, which adds up, overall, to the agreed total length. As you write, compare your output with the planned or target lengths.

Don't think of your word budget as cast in stone, though. It is only a target. Some chapters will inevitably run out over-length and others will be short. As long as the running total is about right, small variations (10% up or down, say) are unimportant. But if chapter after chapter is longer than planned, you must do some serious thinking. Are you waffling? Can you trim back at the polishing stage? An over-long (or over-short) book can negate all the financial calculations the publisher made in determining the viability of the book. If you can see no way out of this difficulty (and almost any writing can be cut back, usually with improvement), contact your editor and discuss it as soon as possible.

Counting words lets you check your overall progress too. Are you writing sufficient words per day to meet the delivery deadline? Checking on daily output also acts as a minor spur to achievement.

For day-to-day purposes, the word count provided by your word processor is fine for checking on progress. For a beginner though, I believe that actually counting the words individually is a good way of getting the feel of one's writing style. I counted words one by one for years.

Organising the writing routine

You should try to be regular in your writing habits. Someone who writes only 'when the muse moves them' is an amateur, probably unpublished and likely to remain so. The professional writes steadily and regularly, on good and bad days alike. Regularity helps to keep the words flowing. It keeps the writing muscle exercised and fit.

Some authors write for a set number of hours a day; others set themselves a target wordage. I belong to the latter school.

Writing full-time, I set myself a readily achievable target of 800 words per day on a book project plus all my regular and irregular articles. And, of course, these target output figures exclude the time needed for planning, research, redrafting, and all the business matters associated with authorship. Given the facts more or less at my fingertips, I can now do the first draft of a non-fiction book in about two months. I keep a record of my daily output on the same computer file or sheet of paper as my chapter and book word budget.

A non-fiction author working to the system I advocate in this book – detailed book and chapter synopses and regular writing – should never suffer from . writer's block. Writer's block is when the words just won't come. It's when you don't know where you're going. I believe it is more of a novelist's complaint and then mostly for those writing literary fiction, without the preliminary synopsis used by many genre writers. The worst that should afflict a non-fiction author is inertia.

If you suffer from inertia, having trouble getting started each day, here are some hints:

- Start with an easy section. With a detailed synopsis, there's no need to write in sequence.

- When you finish writing each day, stop in mid-sentence and leave yourself a note of what the next few words are to be. Next day, reread the previous two or three paragraphs and then, with the note, you'll be away.

- If you're really stuck, read what one of the competitive books had to say on your next subject. You can do better than that!

'The professional writes steadily and regularly, on good and bad days alike.'

While actually writing, don't worry overmuch if a sentence won't come right. Write it as best you can and come back to it. You can polish it later. It's more important to keep the flow moving than to perfect one sentence.

Organising the illustrations

Illustrations are important. Just about every non-fiction book, technical and story-line alike, is improved by good illustrations. They are the first thing people look at when they flip through the pages of a book. They may tip the balance in favour of a sale. Illustrations are virtually essential in non-fiction books for children.

However, illustrations cost money and take up space. An American newspaper magnate once said that one good picture was worth a thousand words of print. No doubt that's true, as long as it's a good picture and earns its space. However, some illustrations can cost more than the words they replace.

In random order of importance, the real functions of illustrations in a non-fiction book are:

- To help the reader to visualise something more easily than by reading a description or trying to absorb columns of figures; to make the description 'come alive'.

- To portray a process where, for instance, it would be difficult to describe the concurrence of several activities as clearly as they could be drawn; for example, in a flow chart.

- To break up the text and to relieve the areas of grey print and make the book's pages look more attractive. (Jokey illustrations – cartoons – are sometimes included in relatively serious books for either adults or children to brighten up the overall feel.)

Every illustration should enhance or reinforce the text, not merely duplicate an already adequate description. An illustration should always be informative, if only in clarifying the text.

Most illustrations for non-fiction books will be either line drawings or photographs. Technical books may use line drawings as well as photographs, and story-line books will use mostly photographs. You will have sorted out with the publisher how many illustrations and of what sort.

It is important that, if illustrations are agreed, you think about them while preparing the text. They should be integrated with the text, not added in as an afterthought. Attention should be drawn to them in the text.

Organising your equipment

It is essential for the 21st century non-fiction author to be organised electronically. You must have a computer – either a desktop model or a laptop – a printer and a broadband connection to the Internet.

If you expect to be moving around while working – collecting information, perhaps – then a laptop may be the answer. If you are just sitting at a desk working, then a desktop computer probably makes more sense. Either should cost you well under £500. The computer will usually come with a word processor program (most likely Microsoft Word) included or available separately.

On its own, the computer will not print out your written work i.e. make a 'hard copy'. For that, you need a printer. This can be either an ink-jet printer or a laser printer. Ink-jet printers can be very inexpensive, though they make up for this with the cost of the ink refill cartridges.

If you see no need to print anything in colour, a laser printer is a worthwhile alternative. Not long ago I bought myself a new mono laser printer (Samsung ML-1640) for around £70. Refill cartridges cost virtually as much as the printer, but one usually lasts me about a year.

As emails are increasingly the communication mode of choice, you need to be connected to the Internet. A broadband connection is not difficult to set up. Identify an Internet Service Provider (ISP) – BT, Virgin, TalkTalk, etc – and they will provide everything you need and step-by-step advice on how to do it. A broadband connection will (in 2010) cost you around £20 per month. It enables you to 'surf the web' and to send and receive emails. A broadband connection does not interfere with your telephone line.

If you are new to broadband, don't be scared – it's easier than it sounds (if you get stuck, ask any 14-year-old for help). Once you start using emails, your postage costs will plummet!

But the non-fiction author also needs other, non-electric, equipment:

- A filing system – you should keep hard copies of your research material and your correspondence. Invest in a four-drawer filing cabinet – your writing 'stuff' will quickly expand to fill it.

- A telephone, ideally with answering machine. You must be readily available to your publisher.

- A camera – I would go for a digital single-lens reflex (DSLR). Even if you're not a skilled photographer – and it's not difficult these days – a simple compact camera is an ideal way of recording scenes for writing up later.

- A set of letter scales will save you many trips to the post office. Even with emails, there will still be many occasions when you need to send, say, a weighty book manuscript to the publisher.

- Maybe a pocket recorder if you expect to do many interviews or need to make on-the-spot notes.

Summing Up

- You need to plan out the content of each chapter – its structure and sequence – before you start writing it.

- When writing, bear in mind the delivery date you have agreed to and work at it regularly, not just when you feel like it. Plan on writing a set number of words or for a set number of hours per day. Check your progress against a word budget.

- Many non-fiction books benefit from illustrations, which may be sample pages, diagrams or photographs. Don't leave illustrations to the last minute – work on them as you progress through the book and tie them in to the text.

- You need the right equipment: computer, printer, filing system and telephone are all essential. A camera and a tape or digital recorder will also be useful.

Chapter Six

The Words and Pictures

I can't pretend to teach you how to write. Each person's style is their own. I can do little more than offer a few helpful guidelines.

The first piece of advice about writing style is: don't worry. The non-fiction author doesn't have to write great literature, the sole purpose is to communicate. The most effective non-fiction authors are those whose writing style does not come between them and their readers.

It is easy to advise aspiring authors that the way to write well is to practice. But that doesn't help much. Writing style can also be improved by exposure to good writing – fiction or non-fiction. However, the author of technical type non-fiction books should be wary of the colourful descriptive passages found in some novels. Colourful description may be useful in story-line type non-fiction, but it is seldom appropriate in technical non-fiction.

Effective, readable non-fiction writing is not easy. You have to work hard to produce an easy read. Sheridan got it right:

> *'You write with ease, to show your breeding,*
> *but easy writing's curst hard reading.'*

'I notice that you use plain, simple language, short words and brief sentences. That is the way to write English.'

Mark Twain.

An easy read

While writing style must always be a matter of personal choice, a few guidelines may help:

- Never forget the target reader.
- Be accurate.
- Be brief – keep your writing tight and concise, and don't waffle.

- Be clear – ensure your writing is easy to understand.

The last three are the ABC of writing: A: accurate, B: brief and C: clear.

But the most important thing for the non-fiction author to remember is the target reader. Your purpose is to communicate. If the reader doesn't understand, you're wasting everyone's time.

You must never write down to the reader. A patronising attitude will put anyone off. You must write what the reader wants to read, not what you want to write. Think of your target reader – child or adult – as intelligent but just less aware than you of the particular subject. (You might use simpler words and more explanation when writing for children, but the amount of explanation needed depends solely on where the reader is starting from.)

Think how little you yourself know about mink farming or deep-sea diving. You would want a book on those subjects to start from scratch and carry you along.

Accuracy

The need for accuracy is obvious. A book is 'an authority'. For years, readers will refer to your book, treating its contents as fact, unless it is clearly differentiated as opinion. One silly little mistake can damn an otherwise authoritative volume. The research processes outlined in chapter 2 should guard against inaccuracy – but you must always check and recheck.

The need for accuracy does not stop with the facts though. Are you certain of the meaning of that word? (Check in the dictionary and then replace it with an 'easier' word.) Your target reader won't necessarily have a dictionary handy and strange words disturb the reading flow.

Check your spelling too. (Don't rely on the spellchecker built into your word processor.) A writer's dictionary should be well-thumbed.

Brevity

Brevity is not really the right word – be concise is better. Cut out unnecessary words.

Conciseness is a virtue, but there is room in a non-fiction book to expand. Just take care to ensure that the expansion is neither waffle nor padding. Non-fiction writing has to be taut, yet expansive where detail is necessary. Everyone's writing can be improved by judicious trimming.

Brevity is also applicable to words, sentences and paragraphs:

- Always use a short word in preference to a long word, even if this means using two or three short words to replace one longer one. Use words with which most people are familiar. Short words are easier to understand than long ones. If you absolutely have to use a long or difficult word, ensure that the meaning is made clear by explanation or context.

- Keep sentences short and restricted to a single statement. Aim at an average sentence length of about 15 words and a maximum length of 25 words. (For counting purposes though, treat properly used semi-colons and colons as full stops.) But vary your sentence lengths; don't make them all about the average length. Remember that a 25-word sentence needs a 5-word one to balance out.

I don't criticise long sentences merely because they are long; long sentences can be perfectly clear. But to write a good, long sentence requires skill; it's far easier to write a good, clear, short sentence. And short sentences are easier to punctuate: commas and full stops usually suffice.

- For book paragraphs, work to an average length of about 80 words and a maximum of perhaps 150. (In case you're checking, I tend to use even shorter paragraphs.)

There are two reasons for these length-limits. First, no paragraph should deal with more than a single thought, often introduced in the first sentence and elaborated on in subsequent sentences. This leads to short paragraphs. Secondly, short paragraphs actually look easier to understand – the readers feel more comfortable.

As with sentences, avoid equal-length paragraphs; vary the lengths. An occasional short, 'tabloid-style' paragraph will wake readers up.

As you write, think about your sentence and paragraph lengths. Do your paragraphs look long? You can always divide a long-looking paragraph into two. (The 'rule' about 'one para, one thought' does not preclude such splitting, resulting in 'two paras, one thought'. But avoid 'one para, two thoughts'.)

Many of us let our sentences ramble on. Watch particularly for the mid-sentence 'and', which can often, with improvement, be replaced by a full stop. Also think before you insert that qualifying clause in mid-sentence. Might it not be better as a separate sentence, immediately after its 'parent'?

Think too about the effect of a string of similar sentences. Several short sentences in sequence create an urgent, jumpy feeling (ideal in a thriller, less so in a non-fiction book). A run of long sentences can generate a soporific effect.

Much of the advice in this section relies on counting words. Counting words improves your style.

Clarity

The non-fiction author's purpose is to communicate, to convey information. Thinking of your target reader, your message must be clear and unconfusing.

The best way to write clearly is to write simply. In his book, *The Technique of Clear Writing*, the American guru Robert Gunning recommends that you write like you talk. But take that with a pinch of salt. Many people speak English loosely, some badly. Let's restate it. Write as you wish you spoke – simply, confidently and expressively, using familiar words, but without excess colloquialism.

As you write, think to yourself, 'Would I say it like that? Or would it sound pompous, wordy and unclear?'

A writer must write at the right level for the target reader to understand, but without 'talking down'. Strive for a smooth, non-flowery flow of words and thoughts. If you write like you talk, you will use mainly everyday words. Everyday words are short, simple and easy to understand.

Punctuation too should help to make the writing clear, but don't overdo it. Punctuate only as much as is necessary to make the meaning clear. Long sentences often need a lot of punctuation, whereas most short sentences are already clear and are well served by commas and full stops alone. Advantage: short.

A comma indicates a pause and a full stop indicates the end of a statement. Colons and semi-colons are almost full stops. Semi-colons are used to link two short, closely related but independent statements or to separate items in a list that already contains commas. The colon is used to introduce an idea that is an explanation or continuation of the statement before it. It is also the correct introduction to a list of related items; it should not be followed by a dash.

And to end this brief review of punctuation marks: the exclamation mark should be used extremely sparingly. (Ration yourself to one a month.)

More 'stylistics'

An efficient, transparent, writing style requires more than just brevity and clarity though. The non-fiction author's writing should as far as possible, also:

- Be in the active voice, rather than the passive.
- Be free from unnecessary jargon.
- Flow smoothly.

It is livelier, more direct, to write, 'Gordon Wells wrote this book' than to write, 'This book was written by Gordon Wells'. The first is in the active voice, the latter, passive. Wherever possible, prefer the active voice to the passive.

Be careful with jargon. One person's jargon can be another's everyday technical language. Outright condemnation of jargon is inappropriate; in the right place, jargon is the correct thing to use. It may be useful for the reader to be made aware of the relevant occupational jargon. If so, its meaning must be explained when first used. It is unintelligible and unnecessary jargon that is to be avoided.

The flow of your writing is one of the major elements in an easy read. The earlier recommendations of short sentences and short paragraphs could (if followed too slavishly, without varying their lengths) produce jumpy prose. But varied paragraph lengths alone are not enough to generate a smooth flow: paragraphs should also be linked together.

Paragraph links remind the reader of what has gone before, and show how the next paragraph follows on.

Useful linking phrases include:

- There are other ways…
- Similarly…
- That was not the only…
- Not only does… but…
- Therefore…
- It follows that…
- After that…
- Then…

And don't forget the easy, effective, yet oft-maligned 'old faithfuls': 'And' and 'But'.

The content of the writing

Let's look now at what you will write and how:

- Try to start the book and each chapter with a good 'hook' – something to 'grab' the reader.

- In technical type non-fiction books, consider starting a chapter or section with a bullet point list. Then expand on each item in turn. Once the points are listed, the reader knows what to expect.

- Appeal to the reader's self-interest. Recommend specific courses of action but mention the alternatives too.

Need2Know

- Wherever appropriate, illustrate your writing with examples. Make your words mean something to the reader, For example, it is often clearer to say a lamp standard is as high as a two-storey house, rather than (or as well as) giving its exact measurement. (The standard advice to fiction writers to 'Show, don't tell' is equally valid for the non-fiction author.)

Because you have already prepared your overall synopsis and further developed the content and internal sequence of each chapter, you will always, as a non-fiction author, know what to write next. All you have to do is get on with it.

One final technical writing point on writing numbers. Ask your publisher for his preference and stick to it; consistency is what's important. Also avoid starting a sentence with figures. If you need to, rearrange the words.

Preparing the illustrations

Many non-fiction books are improved by the inclusion of illustrations. While writing, the non-fiction author should always be thinking about the possibility of an illustration. You should select, visualise and/or roughly draw appropriate illustrations and mention them in the text. Say something like: 'For flow chart, see Figure 0.0'.

Make sure that the advice or information given in the text agrees with that shown in the illustration. It's easy to get it wrong when working on illustrations and text at different times. And remember, illustrations need captions.

Few authors are capable of producing finished 'book-quality' drawings. Drawings prepared for any other purpose are unlikely to be suitable for use in a book. Among other reasons, the lines and lettering will probably be too small. Book illustrations should be purpose-made.

If line drawings are agreed by the publisher, you should agree the form in which they are to be prepared and presented. Either finished (unlettered) drawings or rough sketches. The rough sketches (roughs) should not be too rough though. Ideally, they will be correct in every detail and the correct size, but perhaps only in pencil. The publisher's draughtsman will welcome being able to trace – in ink, with the right weight of line – directly from the roughs.

Photographs for use in non-fiction books should usually be:

- Black and white prints – unless the publisher has agreed in advance that colour is acceptable.

- Needle-sharp – poor focusing will detract from the whole book.

- Printed on glossy rather than matt paper.

- Well-contrasted without being 'soot and whitewash'.

- A good size – 200 mm x 150 mm is usually acceptable.

- Full of the subject – i.e. the subject fills the picture.

- Unmounted – but don't try to separate from an existing mount.

It will nearly always be the author's responsibility to arrange suitable photographs for use in the book. Unless taken by the author, the copyright of nearly all photographs belongs to someone else and reproduction has to be paid for. Ideally, you will have agreed how much the publisher will pay in reproduction fees for photographs. Other than commissioned photographs you will be able to get photographs from museums, art galleries, photographic agencies, picture libraries and from commercial firms and government departments (sometimes for free for publicity purposes).

Be careful though: the fact that you have bought a picture-postcard of an exhibit from a museum, art gallery, etc does not give you the right to use it in your book. For that there will be a reproduction fee. Don't pay this at the time of purchase. Ask what the fee will be. If within the pre-agreed budget, the publisher will pay when the picture is needed.

Tables and quotations

Some technical non-fiction books are improved by tables of factual information and many story-line non-fiction books include extensive quotations.

Small tables can be included in the run of text. However, tables larger than three or four lines in depth should be treated as illustrations. That is, not included in the text, but kept separate, numbered, captioned and referred to. Avoid vertical lines in all tables and use space in lieu. Horizontal lines, however, are fine – leave a line-space beneath them.

Quotations of up to about 50 words are usually included in the text itself, indicated by quote marks. Longer quotations (extracts) should not be separated in the same way as illustrations, but included in the run of the text. They should be clearly introduced and, where appropriate, their source mentioned. (In the typescript, separate them by a line space above and below and sideline them with a marginal note, 'quotation'.)

If you include quotations in your book, remember to get permission. Any unauthorised quotation can be an infringement of copyright, though a blind eye is usually turned on those up to about 50 words long. Your publisher may be able to suggest an acceptable form of words for release of copyright for quotations. As with illustrations, the publisher may agree to pay for quotations and will specify an overall figure. Some authors or publishers demand significant fees for sizeable quotations.

Avoid footnotes: they're difficult to set and expensive. Chapter- or book-end notes are more acceptable to publishers but many readers dislike them too, so best avoid them also. Ideally, absorb footnote contents into the main text.

Check, rewrite, polish

Working through the chapters, synopsis item by synopsis item, you'll eventually discover that you've finished the book. Well, no, not actually. Just the first draft. There's a lot to do yet.

First though, heave a sigh of relief. You've broken its back. All your thoughts are down on paper. You've earned a rest.

Now comes the real hard work of authorship – converting your first draft into a saleable book.

Read right through your first draft, from beginning to end. Try not to make any corrections yet, just get the feel of the book. Reassure yourself that it is still the book you intended, and agreed, to write. Watch particularly for repetitions and omissions. You've got to do something about these. Once you've finished reading, delete the repeated sections and write the extra paragraphs to fill the gaps.

'If you include quotations in your book, remember to get permission.'

Now go back to the beginning of the book and read it again in detail, chapter by chapter. As you read, ask yourself whether it's an easy read. Reading aloud identifies the pomposities and the confused thinking. If you find it uncomfortable to read a section aloud or find some phrasing clumsy, it needs rewriting. If you stumble over a long word – change it. Check all facts, figures and dates.

Look carefully at the appearance of the paragraphs. Are some too long? Subdivide. Are too many of the same length? Can you join some together or subdivide again? Does that extra-long paragraph contain more than one thought? Split it up.

Watch too, for over-long sentences. Read each one carefully, then either accept it (as a one-off) or 'go for the and'. (A mid-sentence 'and' can frequently be replaced by a full stop and a capital letter). Check for over-use of favourite words or phrases and for words reused too close together. Change them. Put a shine on your writing and check your spelling.

Summing Up

- Don't write to impress your readers: aim for a simple, easy read.

- Whatever you write must be accurate (and devoid of spelling errors), concise (don't waffle) and clear.

- Use short, simple, familiar words, an average sentence length of about 15 words (and a maximum of about 25 words) and an average paragraph length of about 80 words with a maximum of perhaps 150 words (my personal preference is for rather shorter paragraphs than this).

- Seek to grab your readers' attention at the start of each chapter. Illustrate your writing with examples: e.g. don't just give a measurement, explain it. Check that your writing flows and use paragraph links.

- In 'how to' books, include diagrams, small tables and bullet point lists wherever appropriate. In story-line books, include relevant quotations (up to about 50 words).

- Once written, reread your book. Check spellings, facts, logical sequence, readability and correct any faults. Polish it.

Chapter Seven

Presentation and Delivery

Your book has to be delivered to your publisher as double-spaced typescript plus, increasingly nowadays, the word-processed text on CDs. Some publishers prefer a single-spaced typescript with the disc. Whatever the publisher wants, you provide.

Before printing out your typescript, stop and think. Now is your last realistic chance to check on what you've written. Reread your finished draft in its entirety, straight through from beginning to end, as you would a novel. Try to read the finished draft as one coming new to the book. Does it grab you? Ignoring false modesty, it should make you say to yourself, 'That's really good; I like it; I'd buy this'.

Check for consistency. Did you say something like: 'as explained more fully in Chapter 00'? And did you explain? If not, sort it out. Either scrap the early allusion or add the later explanation and correct the missing chapter number.

Not only must the draft be ready for final printing, so must everything else. When you deliver to the publisher, he wants it complete and ready to go: main text, illustrations, captions, preliminary pages (see overleaf), appendices, bibliographies – the lot. If the package is short of anything, you might just as well not bother. It will sit in the publisher's office, waiting for the missing material to arrive and sections of incomplete typescripts can easily be mislaid.

Delivery of an incomplete typescript will annoy the publisher and his opinion of you will drop a notch or three. If delivery of the missing part is after the deadline, this may prejudice the whole production timetable.

'Try to read the finished draft as one coming new to the book.'

Typescript layout

Book manuscripts must be typescripts. A handwritten manuscript won't even get looked at. (The words manuscript and typescript are commonly interchangeable, though typescript is meant.)

Consistency is most important. The typescript must be consistent throughout, in both spelling and layout. (A consistent misspelling is easily remedied at copy-editing stage whereas a multitude of different spellings is more difficult to deal with.) Varying layouts make counting off the wordage much more of a chore and it would all have to be corrected for typesetting.

Your word processor allows you to choose a preferred font. Avoid mock handwriting and other fancy fonts such as Comic Sans MS or Mistral. Go for one of the ordinary ones: Times New Roman perhaps, or Courier. My own preference is for the Tahoma sans serif font, which I use all the time. I use an 11-point font but if using Times New Roman or Courier, a 12-point font is probably better.

As mentioned earlier, either an ink-jet printer or a (mono) laser printer is fine. You choose. But it is much best if you do the typing yourself as this gives you the chance to correct any small errors.

The whole book manuscript must be printed out on one side only of good quality A4 (297 x 210 mm) paper; 80 gsm (grams per square metre) paper is about the right weight. To repeat, the typing must be double-spaced throughout. This means type a line, miss a whole (not half-space) line space. Do not type quotations or inset material in single-spaced – everything must be double-spaced.

Allow good large margins all round: about 40-50 mm on the left side and 25 mm at top, bottom and right side. These margins are needed for editors' and printers' instructions and notes.

Keep the lines of typescript as near as possible the same length throughout; work to a constant number of lines per typed page too. Don't 'right-justify' – that is, with a straightened-out right edge – your typescript; leave the right edge ragged. Right justification can confuse the typesetter as can 'soft' hyphenating in order to squeeze words in at line ends.

Start each chapter on a fresh page. Type the chapter number a few lines down the page and its title a few lines below that; start the text a further few lines down. Be consistent in your chapter-start layout. If you are using within-chapter headings, leave at least one line space above and below them. Again: be consistent.

I recommend that you type both chapter titles and headings in lower-case letters, starting flush at the left margin. If the publisher wants to use capital letters or centred titles or headings, this is a simple correction that is easier than 'undoing' capitals. Don't underline chapter titles or headings. Once you've finished, mark their 'weight' in the left margin, in pencil – [Chap] for chapter title, [A] for 'first-level' headings and, if you have them, [B] for 'second-level' headings.

Indent the start of all paragraphs by a consistent number of spaces – five is common practice. But do not indent paragraphs at the beginning of each chapter, and beneath each heading. Do not leave a blank line between paragraphs. Underline only those words to be printed in italics. Above all – be consistent. (You will notice that this is not the house style at Need2Know, but it is important that you are aware of all publishers' styles).

All the typescript pages must, of course, be numbered and straight through the whole text (i.e. not chapter by chapter). It is a good idea to put a key word from the title, the author's name and the page number in the top right corner of each sheet (a header) e.g. 'Non-fiction/Wells/00'.

Many publishers have their own house style. Some even specify the typescript layout: number of lines per page, etc. Comply with such specifications if possible – it makes life easier.

Consistency is important, not only in layout but also in word-use, spelling and punctuation. In the absence of any guidance from your publisher, consult *The Oxford Writers' Dictionary* (OUP) and as always be consistent. Note particularly:

- Where there are alternatives, standardise on one. 'Photo-copy' or 'photocopy', 'full stop' or 'full-stop'? You decide, then stick to it.

- Use the -ise spelling rather than -ize.

- Use capitals sparingly. ('A duke' rather than 'a Duke', unless specific, as in 'the Duke of Norfolk'.)

> 'Consistency is important, not only in layout but also in word-use, spelling and punctuation.'

- Omit full stops within groups of initials and after abbreviations; thus WHO, MP, Mr, Ms, Lt-Col Smith. When first using an uncommon abbreviation, give its meaning.

- Use single quote marks (inverted commas) for speech or quotations, reserving double quote marks for secondary use i.e. quotations within speech.

Errors & Omissions Excepted (E & OE)

Your final typescript should look good. With an ink-jet or laser printer, check that you have a spare cartridge – Sod's Law guarantees you will run out mid-book.

'No matter how carefully you have checked, one or two errors will probably creep in.'

You will probably need to produce three full sets of typescript, etc (two for the publisher, one for you). File your set in a hole-punched binder. Read it carefully: check for missing lines, spelling errors, missing cross references and, of course, any major omissions.

No matter how carefully you have checked, one or two errors will probably creep in. If these are merely the odd typo, correct the typescript in ink.

If there are major faults – and there shouldn't be if you've done your job properly – you'll have to retype and reprint as necessary.

With a word processor, it's worth reprinting a whole chapter to accommodate insertions or deletions. Adjust the page numbering at the end of the reprinted chapter. If the new chapter has fewer pages than the original, add a note on its last page saying something like, 'Pages 86-88 cancelled, page 89 follows.'

If the new chapter is longer, your job is slightly more difficult. When you reach the last 'available' page number, number it 'Page 88a' and continue with 'Page 88b', '88c', etc. At the foot of page 87, add a note saying something like, 'Additional pages inserted, numbered 88a-88c. Page 89 follows Page 88c.' And on page 88c, add a note saying, 'Next, Page 89.'

Once all copies of the typescript are complete and correct, go through them and mark the preferred locations for illustrations, tables, etc. Write [Fig 1.1] or [Table 23] in the left margin, in pencil, and rely on the printer to bring them in as close as possible to that. (And, as already mentioned, mark the weight of headings, etc in a similar fashion.)

Prelims and end matter

The typescript of a novel only needs a title page, whereas a non-fiction book requires rather more: the contents pages, appendices perhaps, occasionally a bibliography and usually an index. The non-text pages at the front of a book are called preliminary pages or prelims and the extra pages at the end are known as end matter. The non-fiction author has to provide at least some of them.

The first few prelims in a non-fiction book are more or less standard:

Page (i)   Half-title. Always a right-hand page (recto). On it, only the book title.

Page (ii) Half-title verso. The reverse (verso) of the half-title and thus always a left-hand page. What goes here is the publisher's decision. It might be a list of other books by you or by others in the same series.

Page (iii) Title-page. Always a right-hand page. The book's full title, with subtitle, if any; the author's name; and the publisher's imprint/logo, or name.

Page (iv) Title-page verso. The reverse of the title-page and thus always a left-hand page. This page is used for legal and bibliographical requirements: the publisher's name and address, the copyright notice and author's moral right assertion, the book's publishing history, the ISBN and the printer's name.

Page (v)   Contents. Conventionally, these begin on a right-hand page. Details of the contents page are outlined below.

From the contents page onward, the prelims vary from book to book. Your publisher will probably welcome being provided with typed draft prelims for the above.

The contents page should be prepared from the typescript and be an exact replication of at least the titles of chapters and end matter. For technical non-fiction books, the contents page may include the within-chapter headings too, again appearing precisely as in the typescript. Story-line non-fiction books occasionally include similar expansions of the chapter contents. Discuss this with your publisher.

It is helpful to mark, in pencil, on the contents page, the typescript page numbers of chapter starts. But make it clear that these are typescript pages.

End matter is less standardised than the prelims. It may consist of some or all of the following: appendices, endnotes (instead of footnotes), bibliography (or reading list), and, most importantly, the index.

In a bibliography, refer to books by (in order): author's name, book title (underlined for italics, not in quotes, plus edition number), and the publisher's name in parenthesis. List the books alphabetically by author. In formal bibliographies, the author's name is written surname first. In reading lists, the author's name is often shown conventionally.

'The captions are often one of the first things a potential purchaser notices in the book.'

Presenting the illustrations

You have all the illustrations – photographs, finished drawings or roughs. (It is wise to have copies of the photographs and to make photocopies of all the drawings or roughs for your records.)

Every illustration needs a caption. It should state what the illustration is of, it should not be too long (say 25 words maximum) and must be self-contained. The captions are much read. They are often one of the first things a potential purchaser notices in the book. It is important to get them right.

Type the captions, double-spaced and in order, in list format, numbered to correspond with the illustrations. Include the list of captions in with, but separated from (a paperclip will suffice), the rest of the typescript.

Do not, on any account, interleave – or even worse, stick – the illustrations into the typescript.

Illustrations should be carefully numbered and packed in a folder, separate from the typescript. (I use a clear plastic wallet, open at top and one side.) Normally, number all illustrations, irrespective of type, consecutively by chapter. Thus: Fig 1.1, Fig 1.2, Fig 1.3, Fig 2.1, Fig 3.1, etc. Use light soft-pencilled numbers on the back of photographs, or in the front corner of line drawings or roughs.

Keep drawings and roughs separate from the photographs in the folder; it's often a good idea to interleave photographs with thin paper for protection. A clearly identified extra copy of the caption list makes a good list of 'illustrations enclosed'.

Delivery to the publisher

Your book manuscript is at last complete. All the pages (including end matter) are numbered consecutively and the prelims are numbered in a separate sequence. You have the necessary number of copies. Any necessary copyright approvals have been granted and release documents are on your files. Everything is ready.

Don't put the publisher's copies of the typescript in fancy binders. Don't staple pages together by chapter. Don't punch a hole in the corner and insert a Treasury tag. Just bundle everything up (prelims, main text, end matter, caption list, illustrations) with an elastic band around it and put each set (copy) in a strong cardboard wallet. Stick an identifying label on the wallet: Title – author – 'Top'/'Second' copy.

I usually include a list of what is in each wallet: prelims, main text (376 sheets), caption sheet, draft index and five illustrations (in separate folder). I also add a note of any particular editorial requirements. (Keep this minimal though, publishers don't like being told how to do their job.) I also explain the marginal notes on the heading hierarchy.

Delivery will be on or before your deadline. You agreed to work to this date; if you were unlikely to meet the deadline – even by working nights – you should long ago have forewarned the publisher and agreed a revised delivery date. Delivery should be by post. (If you really must deliver by hand, just hand it in and go.) Depending on your state of nerves, you may feel the need to post the two typescripts in separate packages. It is worth using the Recorded Delivery system for the package containing the illustrations.

Delivery on electronic media

Many publishers nowadays also require the book manuscript on CD. As you will have written your book on your computer, delivery in such a way is not a problem.

You will have written your manuscript using one of the usual word processors, almost certainly Word; many publishers are happy with manuscripts delivered in those programs. All you have to do is make an extra copy of your files. It is worth checking with the publisher first though – there is always the possibility of them preferring your manuscript in Rich Text Format (RTF).

You should have written your book as separate chapters each saved as separate computer files. This is much more manageable than one huge file of the whole book. It helps both you and the publisher if you use understandable titles for the files. My files for this book are all called WNFB (the book title in brief) and the chapter number, making this file WNFB-C07.

Delivery of the manuscript on CD means a big saving on postage costs when mailing work abroad. The disc alone will not be enough, but the publisher will often be content with a lighter, single-spaced hard copy.

Starting on the index

I always submit a draft index with the book manuscript, if for no other reason than to indicate the book space that will be required. And you've got to do it sometime (please note, Need2Know's house style requires no index).

Work through your copy of the finished manuscript and highlight (or underline in coloured ink) everything important that may need to be referred to. You will need to mark virtually every chapter title and heading; similarly in technical non-fiction books, mark checklists, illustrations, etc. In story-line books, each mention of every significant person should be identified. It is sometimes useful to make a marginal note of a descriptive phrase that is not in the text, and mark that for indexing. You might, for instance, describe this paragraph as 'highlighting index items' as an index item.

Many word processor programs have facilities for indexing, though I prefer to make my own. I set up a table consisting of one column and many rows, and then type in the marked index items (complete with manuscript page). Remember to repeat entries where appropriate e.g. 'word budget' and 'budget, word'. When the table is complete, the program will rearrange it in alphabetical order. Subject to sorting out of multiple entries, the index is virtually done.

If you don't feel up to doing the index using the computer, you can do it manually – it's just more tiresome. One way is to list all the marked index items on A4 sheets marked with the letters of the alphabet. (Group less-used letters – IJK, PQ, UV, XYZ – together on single sheets.) When all are listed, it is then not too onerous a task to put each letter-list into its own alphabetical order, ignoring word splits. From these reordered letter-lists, you can then prepare the complete draft index.

If the whole idea of making your own index feels beyond you, there are professional indexers who will do the job for you at a price. See the help list for contact details for the Society of Indexers.

Summing Up

- Deliver your book to the publisher as a double-spaced typescript, usually accompanied by an electronic version on CD. Before producing the final typescript, check your work once again.

- The typescript must be on one side only of white A4 paper. Allow wide margins all around. Use a normal font at 11- or 12-point size. Standardise your layout: no spaces between paragraphs; indent all paragraphs consistently (except those immediately beneath headings); reserve underlining exclusively for words to be printed in italics; start each chapter on a fresh page; number pages throughout, not by chapter.

- Provide the preliminary pages (the prelims) and, if required, a draft of the index.

- Provide all the illustrations (numbered) together with the typescript, not 'to follow'. Also provide captions (double-spaced and numbered) for all illustrations.

- Deliver the complete material to the publisher as loose sheets neither stapled nor bound, and preferably in a clearly labelled card or plastic wallet. If a CD has been asked for, provide this at the same time.

Chapter Eight

From Typescript to Book

You have delivered your book to the publisher. What now?

Your editor – in the role of commissioning editor – will read it right through herself. She will probably ask someone else, a specialist perhaps, to read it too. They will check first for understandability and then for accuracy, coverage and accidental omissions.

Immersed in writing about your subject, and knowing it so well, it is easy for there to be a slight falling off of understandability without you noticing. The editorial check-reading is therefore greatly to your advantage. If an editor or a specialist finds it hard to understand then so too will the beginner – the target reader.

Following that check-reading, you may be asked to rewrite one or more sections of the book. Don't be worried or upset by such requests (so long as they are not too extensive). Small rewrites are not at all unusual and are usually beneficial. Even if the changes asked for are extensive, as long as you accept that they are sensible, they are worth making. If not, talk to your editor – convince her that she is wrong.

Literary pride is inappropriate: if a small rewrite will improve your book then get rewriting. Rewrites done, the commissioning editor should now be satisfied with your manuscript. (I once rewrote an opening chapter three times before the publisher was content and the book was much better as a result.) You may have had to change the sequence of some chapter sections – a 'cut-and-paste' job, easy on the computer – or maybe there were no changes at all. Anyway, it's now accepted.

The manuscript moves next to the copy editor who, in smaller publishing houses, can be the same person wearing a different 'hat'. Commissioning and copy editors have different roles.

'Small rewrites are not at all unusual and are usually beneficial.'

Meanwhile, the second copy of your book manuscript may have gone to the production staff to get cost estimates from printers, etc. It may also be shown to potential purchasers of foreign rights.

Copy-editing

The copy editor is concerned with the quality of your manuscript rather than its content. The copy editor's task is to check your manuscript in detail for sense, consistency, grammar, syntax, spelling and punctuation. She will also check compliance with the publisher's house style and prepare the typescript for despatch to the typesetters and printers.

'The copy editor's task is to check your manuscript in detail for sense, consistency, grammar, syntax, spelling and punctuation.'

Copy editors are individuals, all different. Some seem to delight in making many stylistic changes to a non-fiction author's text; others are content merely to correct faults while leaving the style undisturbed. Ask for sight of your edited manuscript before it is sent to the printers. You can then check that no harm has been done to your work.

Most non-fiction authors have a love-hate relationship with their copy editors. I have a rather casual writing style seldom approved of by the more pedantic copy editors. Against that, several of my books have benefited from sympathetic copy-editing: correcting my occasional faults.

Criticism apart, copy editors meet an essential need and all authors should be grateful for their skill. But copy editors cannot be expert in every speciality; you must check that they do not inadvertently change the sense of your words. (Another reason for you to see the edited typescript.)

The copy editor also prepares the typescript for typesetting. This entails adding instructions for the typesetter: fonts to be used in headings, spaces between text and bullet point lists, etc. A good-looking printed page doesn't happen by accident.

Proofs

Once the copy-editing is complete – and hopefully checked by you – the marked-up typescript goes off for typesetting. Eventually, and it always seems a long time, you will receive a set of proofs for correction. With the proofs you may also get the original marked-up typescript.

The proofs will almost certainly be page proofs that reflect the final appearance and pagination of the book. They will be on A4 paper, but with page borders indicated. Illustrations may not always be included in the page proofs but space will have been left for them.

Proofs are for the checking of the layout and typesetting. They are not an opportunity to change your mind or improve your explanations.

With more and more authors delivering their work on disc, in the form of output from the major word processor programs, manuscripts are seldom retyped. Typographical errors in the proofs are therefore likely to be the author's own. But occasional glitches do slip in. (And I swear they're not mine, guv.)

Apart from carried-over author's typos to be corrected, there can be unfortunate page-breaks, causing unsightly 'widows' or 'orphans' (single, sometimes short, lines at the top or bottom of the printed pages). You should check for these and for other typesetting errors: wrong fonts (italic instead of roman, for example, or the reverse) or incorrect heading weights.

Watch out too for incorrect or missing running heads (if used) and incorrect chapter titles on the contents page (particularly a different use of capital letters). Are all of the illustrations included – or space left for them – and in an acceptable position? You must also now correct the previously unknown page numbers that you showed in the typescript as '00'.

Because you wrote the book and know its content backwards, there is a danger, when proofreading, that you will skim-read and not spot the errors. Be extra careful.

When you find something that needs correcting, be sure to mark it using the standard notes and symbols. These (from British Standard BS5261: Part 2) can be found in the annual *Writers' & Artists' Yearbook* and by searching online. It is particularly important that not only are the errors marked in the

'Proofs are for correcting not for mind changing.'

text, but also with the appropriate mark in the margin. (The typesetter checks the margins and no marginal note can mean no correction.) Use red ink for correcting printer's errors, and black or blue ink for author's corrections. The printer will not charge for correcting his own mistakes but will certainly charge the publisher for all your changes.

And beware – your agreement will permit the publisher to deduct the cost of excessive author's corrections from your royalty account. 'Excessive' arrives sooner than you might expect. Keep author's corrections to an absolute minimum.

Despite those warnings, you must not allow your own errors of fact to remain uncorrected. (Sod's Law guarantees that no matter how carefully you have checked your typescript, some factual error will have slipped through.) Correct this but, as far as possible, maintain the existing number of characters. If you delete a word or phrase, replace it with some innocuous padding. If you need to add words, search for something of equal length that can be deleted.

You may also have to answer typesetter's queries. (These will be in the margin, ringed, and probably in green ink. If the answer to a query is 'yes', cross out the question mark; if the answer is 'no', delete the whole query and write the correction in the margin. 'OK' alone can be ambiguous.) If you make any comments, keep them brief – the printer doesn't want to read an essay.

The proofs must always be dealt with quickly. Although your agreement may allow you two or three weeks, you will probably be asked to turn them round within days. This is not the time to ask a colleague for an opinion. Burn the midnight oil; get them right and do it quickly.

You may find this proofreading checklist helpful:

- Have you answered all the printer's queries?

- Are all your author's corrections essential?

- Have you used standard proofreading marks?

- Are your corrections, explanations or notes for the printer clear, legible and brief?

- Have you corrected all page, illustration or chapter numbers in the references and on the contents page?

- Have you balanced out deletions and additions?

- Have you checked for missing or repeated lines and passages?

- Are all illustrations acceptably located and do their numbers and the text references to them agree? Check the captions too.

- Are the running heads present, correct and on the correct page – book title on left, chapter title on right?

- Do chapter titles – and heading titles if included – on the contents page agree with those in the text? (Check capitals particularly.)

You should have been sent two copies of the proofs – one set to send back and one for your retention. Before you return the corrected set, mark up your own copy to match. You will use this set to complete the index – see below.

You will not, usually, be the only person checking the proofs. Almost certainly your editor will also read them and make her own corrections. When she gets your corrections, they will be collated with hers before returning to the printers. The editor may override some of your suggestions.

Completing the index

Your index should already be half done. From the page proofs, it can be completed. Referring to your original, highlighted typescript, mark up the page proofs to match. All the indexed items will then be highlighted in the page proofs.

Now, with the typescript, proof copy and draft index, correct the index page numbers. Work slowly through the page proofs. As you come to a colour-marked word or phrase, check it against the typescript, find the entry in the draft index and correct the page number. I suggest crossing out the typescript page number and replacing with the proof page number. When you get to the last page, check for any typescript page numbers that haven't been crossed out and rectify.

From your now accurate index, either correct the proof index or provide a new, correct, typescript. The whole process should take no more than a few hours.

If you didn't produce a draft index based on the typescript, you have to go through the same process described in chapter 7, but on the page proofs. The recommended approach gives a quicker turnaround at proof stage.

Most of my indexes have no more than 350-400 entries. However, some story-line books may need a more comprehensive index: names of many people and places, book and magazine reference titles, etc.

For more complicated indexes, you might need to employ a professional indexer. Contact the Society of Indexers. (In that situation, I would strongly recommend trying to persuade your publisher to meet the not insignificant cost.)

It is unlikely that you will see proofs of the finished index; the editor herself will probably check it – there is seldom time at that stage for consultation.

The book arrives

Eventually, usually about 12 months after you delivered your manuscript-baby to the publisher, the book will be published.

The printer should deliver copies to the publisher about four to six weeks before the official publication date to allow for distribution. You may receive your complimentary copies at the same early date.

At last you have your book in your hand. Almost certainly, you will be delighted with it. You will read it through proudly and almost inevitably discover a tiny misprint that you didn't notice in the proofs. You wonder what the reviewers will make of the book.

As publication day approaches, you grow more and more excited. But there won't be a book launch party. You won't be on a TV chat show. There won't be a review in *The Sunday Whatsit*. If anyone sends you a bunch of flowers, it'll probably be your partner. Don't worry: it happens to all of us.

What about the complimentary copies? You will get anything from six to 24 and many requests for free copies. I keep one copy of each book in pristine condition – hardly opening its pages – as my archive copy. I use another as my working copy. I refer to it frequently and annotate it with amendments and notes for a possible further edition. If anyone has helped me with advice or comments, I usually give them a signed copy. Maybe a copy for whoever sent you the flowers. And, usually, that's all.

You're now a published non-fiction author.

Summing Up

- The publisher will read your work in detail and may come up with clarification queries. Deal with these swiftly. A copy editor will also check your work for sense, consistency, grammar, spelling and punctuation, and prepare the work for typesetting.

- You will receive proofs of the book pages for checking. These are for correcting, not for mind changing. Where any errors have to be corrected, you should try hard to maintain the same number of characters as in the original. Check your proofs as swiftly as possible – you will probably be allowed 10-14 days maximum.

- Now that the book is in page proof, you should complete the index (if required). This task is not difficult, but if necessary you can enlist the services of the Society of Indexers.

- You may have to wait up to 12 months from manuscript delivery to publication day. There will not be a book launch party, unless you do it yourself. There will not be dozens of reviews in the daily press. But you are now a published author. Enjoy.

Chapter Nine

Business Matters

For the moment, the writing work is done. There's time to stand back and think about the non-writing aspects: the business matters. They are an important part of the professional attitude to writing.

The agreement has already been mentioned. It is central: it commits both author and publisher to the project.

The agreement

Most publishers have standard printed forms for their agreements, with built-in provision for variation in some areas. Most are based on a specimen contract produced by the Publishers Association; some are negotiated with the Society of Authors and the Writers' Guild and incorporate minimum terms (the Minimum Terms Agreement: see later in this chapter). The legal wording of the more-or-less standard clauses in a publisher's agreement is appropriate to the publishing business. Don't ask your high street solicitor to check it for you. It's not their world.

Members of the Society of Authors – you can join once your first book is accepted – can have their agreements professionally vetted by the Society free of charge.

Find an opportunity to discuss the agreement with your commissioning editor before it is prepared. Even the standard printed clauses are not cast in stone; if you have good reasons for requiring sensible changes, these can usually be accommodated. (Don't ask for doubled royalty rates though!)

The most important parts of the agreement to most ordinary (as opposed to big name) non-fiction authors are:

- The book length and delivery date.

- The commitment to publish.

- The royalty rates and advances.

You will have discussed with the publishers and agreed on how long the book is to be. This figure will appear in the agreement, committing you to that length. The importance of keeping to the agreed book length has already been explained. If you think you are in danger of under- or over-running, you must discuss this with your editor.

Some agreements specify the length in words (plus number of illustrations), others in book pages. Book pages can usually be translated at about 350-400 words per page, but remember to allow for the illustrations too.

The delivery date is as important as the length. You will have discussed this too with the publisher: don't agree to a delivery date that you cannot meet. The delivery date is in the agreement and you are committed to it. Again if, for a really good reason, it looks like you're going to be late delivering, let the publisher know as early as possible. (You shouldn't deliver too early either.)

Both author and publisher are parties to the commitment to publish. You are committed to delivering an acceptable manuscript and the publisher is committed to publishing the book and paying the agreed royalties. The author warrants that the material is accurate and original, does not infringe anyone's copyright and is neither obscene nor blasphemous. The author confirms that he/she has not written, and agrees not to write, any competing works without the prior agreement of the publisher. The publisher is committed to publishing the book wholly at his own expense, and 'within a reasonable time'. (Better agreements specify publication within x months after delivery.)

'If, for a really good reason, it looks like you're going to be late delivering, let the publisher know as early as possible.'

Royalties

Most writers are paid on the basis of their book sales – royalties. Royalties are usually a percentage of the book's selling price and are paid in arrears. An advance is just that: an advance payment against as-yet-unearned future royalties. Thereafter, royalties are not paid until the advance has been recouped.

The financial arrangements for every book are unique and may be negotiable. Royalty rates of 10% of the published price for home sales of hardback books and 7.5% for paperback books are more or less standard.

Variations are legion though: mass market paperbacks sometimes pay 5% of list price – or less – but the sales are potentially much larger.

Royalties for overseas sales and special deals have a different basis: often 10% of the net price received. Some publishers offer home sales royalties (sales made in the UK) too, based on receipts. This simplifies their calculations. The royalty rate paid to the author should compensate for this payment basis: if the publisher sells a paperback book at a not unusual discount of 50%, the royalty rate paid to the author needs to be 15% of price received.

An agreement may include provision for the basic royalty rate to increase when sales exceed a specified figure. At that point, the royalty rate might increase by 2.5%; sometimes a second royalty jump will be provided for. But don't hold your breath: many books never reach the royalty jump figure.

Royalties are usually paid once or twice a year and customarily three months after the period on which they are based. If royalties earned do not exceed the advances paid, you will get an account but no cheque. If the royalties earned are less than a certain amount, payment may be held over to the next accounting period. The accounting periods and payment dates are specified in the agreement.

Advances

Non-fiction authors should expect a payment in advance, on account of future royalties. Most publishers will pay such an advance, but 'royalty-only' deals are no longer uncommon.

Non-fiction authors – of whatever type of book – seldom receive massive advances. Few publishers would offer much less than a £500 advance nowadays and a £2,000 advance for a technical non-fiction book would probably be generous. Story-line non-fiction books tend to attract the larger advances.

A middle-of-the-road non-fiction advance would be half the royalty earnings of the initial print run. Thus: the advance for an £8 paperback on 7.5% royalty and a 2,000 print run might be:

$$0.5 \times 2000 \times 0.075 \times £8 = £600.$$

If a publisher pays you a larger-than-usual advance, he will push the sales harder to recoup his outlay. There is also the 'bird in the hand' justification for seeking as large an advance as possible. Ask. They can always say no. Bear in mind too that the advance may be all you get. Not all books sell sufficient copies for the royalties to 'earn out' the advance. And, the advance is non-returnable.

The advance is usually paid in parts, at any or all of the following points:

- On signature of the agreement.
- On delivery (or acceptance) of the complete manuscript.
- On publication of the book.

Experienced non-fiction authors can hope for the advance payments to be 'front-end-weighted', whereas new authors must expect less on signature and/or delivery, and more on publication. There is only one advance: the stage payments are merely part-payments.

Not all non-fiction books are commissioned on a royalty basis, although this is vastly to be preferred (by the author). Some publishers – including many of children's non-fiction – only offer lump sum payments to the author. Book packagers too often work on a lump sum basis.

The disadvantage of even a generous lump sum payment is, of course, that the author will have no share in a book's future success. But there's seldom any choice – it's either a lump sum or no commission.

Other agreement clauses

Other agreement clauses of interest, but possibly limited importance, include:

- You indemnify the publisher against any infringement of copyright by you.
- You will have to meet the cost of excessive corrections.

- You will be given a number of free copies of your book – seldom less than six, seldom more than 20 – and will be allowed to buy further copies at trade discount. (These are supposedly 'not for resale', but a blind eye is usually turned. You can also often buy one-off copies of books by other authors at a similar discount.)

- You will often be expected to offer your next book to the same publisher, usually on the same terms. Some dislike this clause on the grounds that it is a valueless restriction of the author. On balance, I would accept it, qualified by 'the next book of the same type' and 'at terms to be mutually agreed'.

- There will be clauses about subsidiary rights. These are seldom of importance for UK-oriented technical type non-fiction books; they might be for a story-line type book. You will know. If in doubt, the advice of the Society of Authors or the services of a literary agent may be helpful.

- There will be a clause dealing with the termination of the agreement. This clause should enable you to claim the reversion of the publishing rights in the book when the publisher thinks it has run its course and does not intend to reprint it. You can then offer the book to another publisher, as a new edition. (This can be a realistic proposition: it has worked for me.) There should be no question of any payment (or repayment) for the reversion of the rights.

- There may be a clause authorising the publisher to hold back payment of part of your royalty earnings against unsold copies being returned. This withholding will be for a specific period – the first year maybe.

Remember: many of the clauses in an agreement can be varied. If you don't like a clause, discuss it and ask for it to be changed. The worst you can get is a no.

'If you don't like a clause, discuss it and ask for it to be changed. The worst you can get is a no.'

The Minimum Terms Agreement (MTA)

The Society of Authors and the Writers' Guild of Great Britain have for several years been seeking to persuade publishers to amend the 'standard' terms to favour the author more.

The MTA seeks to reach – but does not always achieve – agreement on such matters and terms as:

- A limit to the period for which the agreement is valid.

- Once the advance has been 'earned out', no delay in passing on earnings from subsidiary rights, etc.

- The author to be told the size of the print run.

- The author to be involved in consultative discussions about the book's jacket/cover, blurb, illustrations, publicity and publication date.

- No alterations being made to an author's typescript without the author's agreement.

- Minimum royalty rates and 'jumps'.

- Minimum payment rates for sales of subsidiary rights.

Agents

With all these clauses in the agreements, should a non-fiction author employ a literary agent?

Undoubtedly, an agent can negotiate more skilfully and sometimes persuade a publisher to offer an author better terms. Agents can also sometimes 'feed' a non-fiction author with work. Agents often know what new series publishers are planning and they also know the individual skill areas of their authors; it is part of their role to bring the two together.

Almost certainly, a story-line type author will benefit from having an agent if you can find a good one to take you on.

Unfortunately though, few technical authors earn enough to make it worth an agent's while. But then, if you are going to write *Writing Non-fiction Books* or *The Compleat Widget* or the like, you don't really need an agent – the relevant publishers are few and easily identified. Certainly, you would be hard pressed to find an agent willing to take you on.

The publisher's questionnaire

At some time, while you are writing your book, the publisher may send you a questionnaire intended to help with sales promotion and publicity. You should therefore be as helpful as possible. After all, who knows your book better than you?

Typical questions/requests in such a questionnaire:

- Describe the reader(s) you had in mind while writing the book. Specify their job and responsibilities, or their interests. (Easy – we defined our target reader in chapter 3 and in the sales package.)

- Describe your book in a single sentence: say what it will do and for whom. (This is particularly important. Work at it.)

- Describe your book, as to a potential reader, in about 200 words. (This too is in your sales package.)

- How will your book meet a previously unmet need? (Again, see your sales package.)

- List competing books and explain how yours is better. (Sales package again.)

- List the magazines likely to review the book. (Reviews usually generate more sales than advertisements.)

- Can you suggest any well-known people in your field who would read your book before publication and endorse it for publicity purposes? (A cover-quote from a 'name' can boost sales.)

- Describe yourself, and your credentials for writing this book, in about 200 words. (Again, see the sales package.)

And, if the book is a textbook...

- Specify the examination syllabuses for which your book is relevant.

Your answers to the questionnaire will be part of the briefing of the sales force; they won't read the book itself, but they will quote your answers widely and sound knowledgeable.

The blurb

The blurb is the immediate and ever-present sales pitch at the potential book buyer. It is the description on the back cover of a paperback or on the jacket of a hardback book. Its purpose is to explain just what the technical type of book will do for the reader and what it's all about. For the reader of a story-line type of book, it has to give a taste – the all-important flavour – of what's in store. It has also quickly to establish the author's credentials. Its importance can hardly be over-emphasised; it may be all that's read – or it may lead to a sale.

There are considerable skills entailed in writing a successful blurb. It will usually be written by someone fairly senior in the publisher's editorial team in consultation with the sales manager.

Much of what's in the blurb will come from material the author has provided – either in the aforementioned questionnaire or in answer to a specific request for a biography, for instance, or in discussion. Occasionally, a non-fiction author may be invited to produce a draft blurb; they will often be invited to check or factually approve what someone else has written. The author will seldom have the last word though – it has too important an influence on sales to come.

'The blurb is the immediate and ever-present sales pitch at the potential book buyer.'

Against the possibility of being asked for a draft blurb for your book, study the blurbs on up-to-date competing and similar books. For technical type books, blurbs can with advantage use bullet point lists – listing how the book will help or improve the reader. And, while it is important to avoid suggesting that the book contains or will do something that it doesn't, it is essential not to play down what it does offer. For story-line books, the blurb needs to be more literary, more 'continuous', describing some of the more important occurrences that the book deals with. But whether technical or story-line, keep the blurb down to 200 words unless advised otherwise.

The author's biography that customarily appears adjacent to the blurb should always, for all types of book, be short – 50 to 100 words is usually about right – and relevant to the book. If the book is about your hobby, few will want to know about your daytime profession or your domestic arrangements. The biography should laud your achievements in widget collecting or rock-climbing or whatever. It should make clear your credentials for writing that particular book.

Need2Know

Whether invited to or not, it is worth trying to write a blurb and biography for your book. Write the blurb particularly early on in the writing period; doing so concentrates the mind and will help the rest of the writing.

The sales campaign

It is the publisher's business to sell your book. Be prepared to assist in the sales campaign and perhaps offer occasional suggestions, but don't try to teach the publisher his job.

The main sales effort will come from the publisher's sales force. There will be a team of representatives – sometimes in-house, sometimes an outside firm – who will visit booksellers seeking sales. The sales force will not be selling your book alone; they have a whole range of books to offer the bookseller and all in a very short time (minutes rather than hours). It is because the reps have to 'make their pitch' in a minute or so per book that they need the one-sentence descriptions and main selling points from the publisher's questionnaire.

Many first-time authors are surprised when their book is not widely advertised. But advertisements – except occasionally in specialist magazines – of general non-fiction books are seldom cost-effective. Reviews of your book will be of greater benefit. Again, this is why the publisher will have asked for details of relevant journals.

There are never as many reviews as the first-time author expects though: the up-market Sundays and daily broadsheets may review a story-line book, but they are most unlikely to review a technical type non-fiction book. Even your local newspaper will probably ignore your masterpiece, unless they have an odd corner they need to fill up. Often, 'reviews' will be no more than a few lines copied directly from the blurb.

You should, however, get a review in at least one of the specialist journals relating to the subject of your technical non-fiction book – you'll probably have to wait several months to see it. Develop a thick skin too: not all reviews will be complimentary. You must hope that most are. (Remember the show-biz saying: 'It doesn't matter what they say, as long as they get your name right.')

Some publishers will run a mail-shot campaign, distributing leaflets to a proven mailing list, seeking direct sales. Not all publishers will do this; it conflicts with the interests of the trade booksellers. Once again, this is for the publisher to decide, not you.

However achieved, sales should be high for a few months after publication then, inevitably, they will fall off quite sharply. The ideal non-fiction book is one that then settles down to a steady, not too small, monthly sales level.

Having made the point that selling the book is the publisher's responsibility, there are ways in which the author can help. If you can write a feature article on a related topic, you can sometimes persuade a magazine editor to mention your book in the by-line and even include an illustration of its cover. If you hear of a seminar or evening class being run on a related topic, tell your publisher: he might be able to arrange a sales display. Now that you are a published author (therefore 'an expert'), you may be asked to give a (paid) talk: be sure to take along copies of your book for sale and for the publicity.

> 'The ideal non-fiction book is one that then settles down to a steady, not too small, monthly sales level.'

Book pricing

Sales do not depend solely on the efforts of the sales force; they are also a function of the book's price. If a book is, or appears overpriced, sales will suffer; if priced too cheap, the publisher makes insufficient profit.

Many first-time authors wonder about where the book reader's purchase money goes and how little the author seems to get. But book publishing is not the 'licence to print money' that some think.

Some years ago, Tim Hely Hutchinson, founder of what became Hodder Headline plc, explained it all. In an article in *The Author,* the quarterly journal of the Society of Authors, in Autumn 1988 he gave a rudimentary breakdown of who gets what. Bearing in mind that different publishers have different ways of allocating the costs and that they will vary from book to book, the breakdown – for a hardback – was:

Booksellers' trade discount	50%
Manufacturing costs	17%
Publishers' overheads (including editorial)	10%

Distribution and marketing	8%
Author's royalties	10%
Publisher's net profit	5%

When viewed like this, the publisher is clearly not the ogre he seems to be. And if the booksellers' discount looks excessive, think again. The above figure was valid in 1988 – today it is even higher, at least 55%. It is a fact of life: the major booksellers have to pay high street rent and rates and meet considerable staff costs and overheads.

Public Lending Right (PLR)

Still on money, the annual distribution of Public Lending Right earnings is an important source of earnings for the non-fiction author.

Each time a book is borrowed from any British public library, that loan is recorded. (In fact, the loans are registered on a regularly changing sample basis and grossed up, but the principle is the same.) The government provides a variable sum of money each year, which is then distributed to all authors whose books have been borrowed from public libraries during the past year. For each single loan, the payment is small – just a few pence – but when this is repeated nationwide, it becomes worthwhile.

In 2009/10 there were over 37,000 registered authors: more than 14,000 authors received no payment at all; 17,000 earned under £100; 360 authors earned more than £5,000. Of those top earners, 250 actually earned much more, but their earnings are capped at £6,600.

Once your book is published, you should register it and yourself for PLR. Write to: The Registrar – PLR, Richard House, Sorbonne Close, Stockton-on-Tees, TS17 6DA. Their website is www.plr.uk.com.

You should also register your published book with the Authors' Licensing and Collecting Society Ltd (ALCS), The Writers' House, 13 Haydon Street, London, EC3N 1DB (www.alcs.co.uk). ALCS collect secondary royalties for writers and pay them directly. For example, money owed from the photocopying and scanning of books in libraries.

Managing your writing income

Whether you write just one book or go on to write many more, you must keep account of your earnings and expenses. Expect a demand for income tax on all your book-writing earnings. If you keep note of your expenses – including those incurred before your book was published – these can be set against the earnings and reduce your tax liability.

A simple record of all receipts and all expenses in a cash book will suffice – at least initially. (Once successful, it may be worth seeking the services of an accountant.)

I record all expenditure twice – once as a straightforward outgoing and then again by category. I classify expenditure under:

- Postage (always a major expense).

- Research (cost of photocopying, specialist books, etc).

- Stationery (it mounts up).

- Travel (ticket costs, or cost/mile for car travel).

- Others (telephone and broadband charges, etc).

Such a breakdown lets me more readily explain and justify my expenses to the tax inspector. Remember: tax avoidance is permissible, but tax evasion is illegal. Never falsify expense claims.

Future work

Your book is published and copies are in all the shops. What now? Are you a one-book wonder or have you caught the writing bug? Maybe you're already thinking of the next book you'd like to write.

That's fine, and not unusual, as long as you have the content in you. The writing bug is virulent. Go back to page one of this book and start the process all over again, but now let your own experience temper my advice. This book has told you how I think it should be done; if your experience now suggests different – make changes. And good luck.

You must also keep up to date on the subject of your first book against the possibility of the publisher requiring a second edition. Here it is worth explaining the difference between an impression or printing, and an edition. If your book sells the whole of the initial print run, the publisher can readily print further copies of the original material, unchanged – or virtually unchanged (minor errors can be corrected). This is a new impression or printing. When the book becomes out-dated and the text is in need of revision, this entails a second edition.

If you are required to prepare a new edition, be thorough. Do not merely add new material: out-dated material and out-dated thinking needs removal; one or two chapters may need a total rewrite. At the same time though, remember that it is a revised edition of the original book, not a brand-new book.

Good luck and best wishes for further successful non-fiction authorship.

Summing Up

- Your high street solicitor is not the person to check your agreement with the publisher. Join the Society of Authors and have it checked for free. Among other things, the agreement commits you to delivering the typescript on time and the publisher to publishing it.

- Most writers will be paid royalties on the basis of their book sales (though some publishers offer a lump sum). You can expect an advance against future royalties – but you won't be paid more royalties until the advance has been cleared.

- For most non-fiction books you will not need – or be able to attract – an agent. Often the likely publishers will be few and you can negotiate directly.

- You will be expected to assist the publisher with the sales campaign for your book. Deal promptly with any publisher's questionnaire, which is to help sell the book.

- Be sure to register your new book for PLR and ALCS earnings. Do not forget to declare your royalties for Income Tax.

Help List

Support for writers

Arts Council, England

www.artscouncil.org.uk
Works to get great art to everyone by championing, developing and investing in artistic experiences that enrich people's lives.

Irish Writers' Centre

www.writerscentre.ie
Supports established and aspiring writers. Offers workshops, lectures, seminars and courses.

Need2Know

Remus House, Coltsfoot Drive, Peterborough, PE2 9JX
Tel: 01733 898103
sales@n2kbooks.com
www.need2knowbooks.co.uk
Need2Know publishes a range of non-fiction books: from health and nutrition, to education, lifestyle and hobbies. Visit the website for further information and to request an information back for submissions

The Society of Authors

www.societyofauthors.org
Tel: 0207 3736642
The Society of Authors provides information and advice to all writers. Today it has more than 8,500 members writing in all areas of the profession. Visit the website for news, events and resources.

Vanity Publishing Info

www.vanitypublishing.info

Run by Johnathon Clifford, this is an invaluable resource providing clear information about vanity publishing. Free advice pack can be downloaded from the website.

Writers' Guild

www.writersguild.org.uk
Trade union representing writers in TV, radio, film and theatre.

Writing courses

The Arvon Foundation

60 Farringdon Road, London, EC1R 3GA
Tel: 0207 3242554
london@arvonfoundation.org
www.arvonfoundation.org
Offers a wide choice of courses. Use the online search facility to find courses near you. A separate section included for young people.

Ty Newydd Writers' Centre

Ty Newydd, Llanystumdwy, Cricieth, Gwynedd, LL52 OLW
Tel: 01766 522811
post@tynewydd.org
www.tynewydd.org
National writers' centre for Wales. List of courses on the website.

Writers' conferences

This is a selection of the better-known weekend and longer conferences:

- NAWG (National Association of Writers' Groups) Open Festival of Writing – weekend, September, annually, Collingwood College, Durham University, Durham, www.nawg.co.uk.

- The Southern Writers' Conference – weekend, June, annually at Earnley, near Chichester, West Sussex. Contact: Lucia White (Secretary), Stable House, Home Farm, Coldharbour Lane, Dorking, Surrey, RH4 3JG. Tel: 01306 876 202.

- The Winchester Writer's Conference – weekend (plus week-long workshops), June, annually at Winchester university, www.writersconference.co.uk. Contact: Barbara Large MBE, The Centre for Reserach and Knowledge Exchange, The University of Winchester, Winchester, S022 4NR. Email: barbara.large@winchester.ac.uk. Tel: 01962 827 238

- The Writers' Holiday (Caerleon) – week-long, July, annually at Caerleon, Gwent, www.writersholiday.net. Contact: Anne & Gerry Hobbs, School Bungalow, Church Road, Pontnewdd, Cwmbran, South Wales, NP44 1AT. Email: gerry@writersholiday.net. Tel: 01633 489 438.

- The Writers' Summer School (Sawnwick) – week-long, August, annually at Swanwick, Derbyshire, www.swanwickwritersschool.co.uk. Contact: Fiona McFadzean (Secretary), 40 Pemberton Valley, Ayr, KA7 4UB.

Other useful contacts

The Association of Authors' Agents

Anthony Goff (President), Davis Higham Associates, 5-8 Lower John Street, Golden Square, London, W1F 9HA
anthonygoff@davidhigham.co.uk
www.agentsassoc.co.uk

Author's Licensing & Collecting Society Ltd (ALCS)

The Writer's House, 13 Haydon Street, London, EC3 1DB
www.acls.co.uk

The Book Trust

Book House, 45 East Hill, London, SW18 2QZ
www.booktrust.org.uk

The Society of Indexers

Woodbourne Business Centre, 10 Jessel Street, Sheffield, S9 3HY
admin@indexers.org.uk
www.indexers.org.uk

Public Lending Right

The Registrar – PLR, Richard House, Sorbonne Close, Stockton-on-Tees, TS17 6DA
www.plr.uk.com

Remember that your local writers' circle will be able to provide a wealth of support. For contact details, see the NAWG website or ask at your local library.

Magazines

The Author

www.societyofauthors.org
Published by the Society of Authors, but available to non-members.

The New Writer

www.thenewwriter.com
Bi-monthly. PO Box 60, Cranbrook, Kent TN17 2ZR

Writer's Forum

www.writers-forum.com
PO Box 6337, Bournemouth, BH1 9EH

Writing Magazine

www.writersnews.co.uk
Warners Group Publications plc., 5th Floor, 31-32 Park Row, Leeds, LS1 5JD

Writers' News

www.writersnews.co.uk
Warners Group Publications plc., 5th Floor, 31-32 Park Row, Leeds, LS1 5JD

Book List

Book Proposals – The Essential Guide
By Stella Whitelaw, Need2Know, Peterborough, 2011.

Writers' and Artists' Yearbook (annual)
A & C Black, London.
www.writersandartists.co.uk.

The Writer's Handbook (annual)
By Barry Turner (ed), Macmillan, Hampshire.
www.thewritershandbook.co.uk.

Writers' Market (annual)
By David & Charles, Devon.
www.writersmarket.co.uk

Writing Romantic Fiction – The Essential Guide
By Jean Saunders, Need2Know, Peterborough, 2011.

The directories for both the *Writers' & Artists' Yearbook* and *The Writers' Handbook* are available to view online via the publisher's websites. You will need to register, though this is free.

Need2Know